PRACTICAL ENGLISH WRITING
新编实用英语写作教程

主　编　代小玲
副主编　曹姗姗　高　明　刘　洁
编　者　代小玲　黄　娟　刘　洁
　　　　曹姗姗　高　明　田恩泽
　　　　肖棠心　倪　媛
主　审　黄　娟

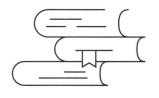

华中科技大学出版社
http://www.hustp.com
中国·武汉

图书在版编目(CIP)数据

新编实用英语写作教程/代小玲主编. -- 武汉：华中科技大学出版社，2021.12(2022.9重印)
ISBN 978-7-5680-7814-6

Ⅰ.①新… Ⅱ.①代… Ⅲ.①英语-写作-高等职业教育-教材 Ⅳ.①H319.36

中国版本图书馆CIP数据核字(2021)第267250号

新编实用英语写作教程 代小玲 主编
Xinbian Shiyong Yingyu Xiezuo Jiaocheng

策划编辑：刘　平	
责任编辑：刘　平	
封面设计：廖亚萍	
责任校对：张汇娟	
责任监印：周治超	
出版发行：华中科技大学出版社(中国•武汉)	电话：(027)81321913
武汉市东湖新技术开发区华工科技园	邮编：430223
录　　排：湖北新华印务有限公司	
印　　刷：武汉市洪林印务有限公司	
开　　本：787mm×1092mm　1/16	
印　　张：10.5　　　　　插页：1	
字　　数：260千字	
版　　次：2022年9月第1版第2次印刷	
定　　价：38.00元	

本书若有印装质量问题，请向出版社营销中心调换
全国免费服务热线：400-6679-118　竭诚为您服务
版权所有　侵权必究

前　言

　　为贯彻《国家职业教育改革实施方案》《职业院校教材管理办法》，落实立德树人根本任务，深化高等职业教育（专科）"教师、教材、教法"改革，根据教育部发布的《高等职业教育专科英语课程标准（2021年版）》的有关要求，本编写组针对高职学生英语写作教学实情编写了该教材，以期提高高职学生实用英语写作水平。

　　本书依据《高等职业教育专科英语课程标准（2021年版）》中基础模块语篇类型及内容要求编写，主要涉及应用文、说明文、融媒体材料三大语篇类型。本书内容新颖，紧贴高职人才培养需求，代表性强；取材在保持整体性和系统性的前提下，凸显了课程标准中关于写作要求中的重难点；书中除介绍常用应用文写作步骤和方法外，还安排了相当数量的范例和练习，供教师和学生参考使用。本书可作为高职英语写作教材供课堂教学或自学使用，也可供企业员工提升个人英文应用文写作水平之用。

　　全书共10章，内容涵盖日常、职场各类常见应用文，如书信、通知、启事、广告、电子邮件、备忘录、简历、日程安排、公司简介、说明书、合同协议等，涉及范围广而且实用性强。每个章节内容按照简介、写作步骤、常用词汇、套用语句、写作范例、练习六个模块进行编写。简介是对本应用文的用途、文本特点、写作注意事项等的简要介绍；写作步骤是教会读者如何一步一步写出规范的应用文；常用词汇和套用语句是小型的语料库，供读者在书写每个步骤时灵活选用；写作范例则是该应用文的完整篇章，读者可以依葫芦画瓢；练习设计由易到难，题目内容涉及写作步骤、套用语句及完整篇章书写等。

　　武汉船舶职业技术学院公共课部基础英语教研室的教师参与了本书的编写和PPT制作工作。其中，代小玲编写第1章第1节至第4节、第8章、第9章及其练习答案，刘洁编写第1章第5至第8节、第10章及其练习答案，曹姗姗编写第1章第9节、第2章、第7章及其练习答案，黄娟编写第1章第10节及其练习答案，田恩泽、肖棠心、高明、倪媛分别编写第3章至第6章及其练习答案。

　　由于编者水平有限，书中疏漏和不当之处在所难免，敬请广大读者批评指正。

编　者
2021年9月

目 录

第1章 信函(Letters) ···1
1.1 感谢信(Letter of Thanks) ···1
1.2 祝贺信(Letter of Congratulations) ··6
1.3 求职信(Letter of Job Application) ···11
1.4 投诉信(Letter of Complaint) ···16
1.5 道歉信(Letter of Apology) ··22
1.6 邀请信(Letter of Invitation) ··26
1.7 询价信(Letter of Inquiry) ···31
1.8 报价信(Letter of Quotation) ···35
1.9 订购信(Letter of Placing an Order) ··40
1.10 推荐信(Letter of Recommendation) ······································45

第2章 通知(Notices and Announcements) ·······································51
2.1 简介(Brief Introduction) ···51
2.2 书面通知(Notices) ···51
2.3 口头通知(Announcements) ··53
2.4 练习(Exercises) ···55

第3章 海报和启事(Posters and Public Announcements) ··················58
3.1 简介(Brief Introduction) ···58
3.2 海报 ···58
3.3 启事(Public Announcements) ··60
3.4 练习(Exercises) ···65

第4章 广告(Advertisements) ··67
4.1 简介(Brief Introduction) ···67
4.2 写作步骤(Writing Steps) ··67
4.3 套用语句(Useful Expressions) ···67
4.4 广告中常见的缩略词(Abbreviations in Ads) ··························68

4.5 写作范例(Samples) ··· 69
4.6 练习(Exercises) ··· 71

第5章 电子邮件(Emails) ··· 73
5.1 简介(Brief Introduction) ··· 73
5.2 写作模式(Writing Model) ·· 73
5.3 基本特点(Basic Features) ·· 73
5.4 套用语句(Useful Expressions) ·· 74
5.5 写作范例(Samples) ·· 74
5.6 练习(Exercises) ·· 76

第6章 备忘录和电话记录(Memos and Telephone Messages) ·············· 79
6.1 备忘录(Memos) ··· 79
6.2 电话记录(Telephone Messages) ·· 84

第7章 简历(Résumés) ··· 89
7.1 简介(Brief Introduction) ··· 89
7.2 写作模式(Writing Model) ·· 89
7.3 基本特点(Basic Features) ·· 90
7.4 套用语句(Useful Expressions) ·· 90
7.5 写作范例(Samples) ·· 93
7.6 练习(Exercises) ·· 95

第8章 说明书(Instructions) ·· 98
8.1 简介(Brief Introduction) ··· 98
8.2 套用语句(Useful Expressions for Instructions) ························· 98
8.3 药品说明书(Drug Instructions) ··· 100
8.4 食品说明书(Food Instructions) ··· 102
8.5 日用品说明书(Necessity Instructions) ···································· 105
8.6 练习(Exercises) ·· 107

第9章 日程和计划安排表(Agendas and Programs) ···························· 109
9.1 简介(Brief Introduction) ··· 109
9.2 写作模式(Writing Model) ·· 109
9.3 写作范例(Samples) ·· 109
9.4 练习(Exercises) ·· 116

第10章 合同和协议(Contracts and Agreements) ······························· 118
10.1 简介(Brief Introduction) ·· 118
10.2 写作步骤(Writing Steps) ·· 118

10.3 常用词汇(Vocabulary) ……………………………………………………118
10.4 套用语句(Useful Expressions) ……………………………………………119
10.5 写作范例(Samples) …………………………………………………………120
10.6 练习（Exercises） ……………………………………………………………127

练习答案 ……………………………………………………………………………130

第1章 信函(Letters)

1.1 感谢信(Letter of Thanks)

1.1.1 简介(Brief Introduction)

　　感谢信是在收到他人赠送的礼物,得到别人的某种帮助或受到别人的款待后写的信。通常要提到对方送的礼物怎么好,帮助有多大,款待得多么周到等。在陈述感谢事由时,应做到客观、准确;在赞扬对方行为时,要恰当、得体,不要过度。该信篇幅无须很长,但要写得热情真挚。

　　此外,感谢信要写得及时,否则,收信人对你的谢意会大打折扣。

1.1.2 写作步骤(Writing Steps)

1) 为某事表达感谢之情。
2) 陈述感谢的具体事由,对被给予的礼物、帮助等进行贴切、诚恳的评价。
3) 再次感谢,或表达回报愿望和美好祝愿。

1.1.3 常用词汇(Vocabulary)

express	*v.*	表达
appreciate	*v.*	感激
gratitude	*n.*	感谢,感激之情
heartfelt	*adj.*	衷心的,真诚的
opportunity	*n.*	机会
truly	*adv.*	真诚地,真实地
sincerely	*adv.*	真诚地,由衷地,诚恳地
faithfully	*adv.*	忠实地,如实地,诚心诚意地
loyally	*adv.*	忠诚地,诚实地

1.1.4 套用语句(Useful Expressions)

表达感谢

1) Thank you very much for.../Many thanks for your...
非常感谢您……

2) I would like to thank you for...
谢谢你……

3) I'm writing this letter to thank you for...
特写此信表达对……的感激。

4) Thank you for taking time and trouble to...
感谢您费时费力……

5) In this letter I would like to convey my heartfelt thanks to...
特写此信表达对您……由衷的感激。

6) I'd like to take this opportunity to express my sincere gratitude to you for...
我想借此机会表达我由衷的谢意,感谢您……

再次表示感谢

1) Thanks again.
再次深表感谢。

2) I do appreciate it.
深表感谢。

3) I appreciate more than I can say.
我感激不尽。

表达美好祝愿

1) Best wishes!
向您致以最美好的祝愿!

2) Best regards to you and your family!
向你和你的家人问好!

3) May the joy and happiness around you today and always.
愿快乐幸福永伴你左右。

4) The best of everything to you.
祝你一切顺利。

5) All the luck in the world to you.
祝您无比幸运。

1.1.5 写作范例(Samples)

Sample 1

January 22, 2021

Dear Susan,

  Thank you very much for your birthday gift of the HUAWEI mobile phone, which I received this morning.

  What a wonderful gift it is! The color is bright, and the design is fashionable. It is really the one I desired. With it, I can learn English, listen to music and watch films…How thoughtful of you to have selected it for me! I'm sure it will be a reminder of our friendship throughout years.

  My heartiest thanks!

Yours sincerely,
Ellen

译文
例1

2021年1月22日

亲爱的苏姗,

  今天早晨收到你送我的生日礼物——华为手机。非常感谢!

  这款手机真是棒极了!它颜色鲜亮,款式新颖,正是我梦寐以求的一款。有了它,我可以学英语,听音乐,看电影……为我挑选这款礼物你真是细心体贴呀!我相信这将是我们多年友谊的纪念。

  真心地感谢你!

你真诚的,
艾伦

Sample 2

February 10, 2021

Dear Mr. Smith,

  I'd like to take this opportunity to express my sincere gratitude to you for your warm try. I would also like to thank you for your interesting discussion with me which I have found

> very informative.
>
> During the visit, my delegation and I were overwhelmed by the enthusiasm expressed by your business representatives. Your hospitality, kindness and courtesies have left a deep impression upon us. I sincerely hope we could have more exchanges like this one when we would be able to continue our interesting discussion on expanding our bilateral economic and trade relations and bring our business people together.
>
> I am looking forward to your early visit to China when I will be able to pay back some of the hospitality I received during my stay in your beautiful country.
>
> With kind personal regards!
>
> Faithfully yours,
> Li Yang

译文
例2

> 2021年2月10日
>
> 亲爱的史密斯先生,
>
> 在访问您美丽的国家期间,感谢您对我和代表团的热情款待,也感谢您和我进行了有趣且有益的讨论。
>
> 在访问期间,我和代表团沉浸在您的商务代表们所表达出的热情之中。您的好客、友好和谦让给我们留下了深刻印象。我真诚地希望我们能有更多这样的交流,以便我们能就双方感兴趣的促进双边经贸关系的问题进一步讨论,并将更多商务人士聚集在一起。
>
> 期盼您早日访问中国,让我们略尽地主之谊,以回报您的热情款待。
>
> 向您致以亲切的个人问候!
>
> 您真诚的,
> 李洋

1.1.6 练习(Exercises)

I. Directions: Finish the letter by choosing the proper sentences given.

A. Again, thank you for the interview and for your time and consideration.

B. The interview strengthened my interest in working for Shell.

C. I enjoyed meeting you and learning more about your research and design work.

D. I would like to thank you for interviewing me yesterday for an associate engineer position in your company.

E. I believe my education and experience in team work fit in nicely with the job requirements, and I'm certain I could make a significant contribution to the firm over time.

October 12, 2021

Dear Mr. White,

_____
_____
_____
_____
_____
_____

Yours sincerely,
Barbara

II. Directions: Fill in the blanks to complete the following letter of thanks according to the given Chinese.

March 24, 2021

Dear Prof. Zhang,

　　_____(感谢您和您的夫人的热情款待) during our visit to your country. We appreciate being introduced to so many of your friends and the delicious Chinese meals we had together. _____(我们在华逗留期间过得非常愉快). We arrived in New York safe and sound yesterday morning.

　　My wife and I are looking forward to the pleasure of playing host to you and your wife in the U.S.A. _____(我们希望有机会回报你们的热情款待).

　　Please do not hesitate to write to me if you want me to do something for you in the U.S.A. _____(向您致以最美好的祝愿)!

Yours sincerely,
Mike

III. Directions: Write a letter according to the situation below.

　　Your friend sent you and your family a New Year present. Write a letter and express your thanks to him/her.

1.2 祝贺信(Letter of Congratulations)

1.2.1 简介(Brief Introduction)

　　祝贺信是一种联络感情的好方式。商务合作伙伴、熟人、朋友或是同事取得了成就,工作业绩受到好评,获得晋升,结婚成家,喜得贵子,周年纪念,开张大吉,乔迁之喜等都是写祝贺信的好机会。祝贺信篇幅不宜过长,一定要写得及时,不然时过境迁,可能失去应有的效果。

　　祝贺信通常包括以下几个方面的内容:叙述事由,表达热烈、诚挚的祝贺;围绕祝贺事件表述贺喜内容;表达美好祝福。在书写主要内容时,可以重点赞扬一下当事人的优秀能力和取得成就的原因,并展望他的美好发展前景。

1.2.2 写作步骤(Writing Steps)

1) 对具体事件表达自己衷心的祝贺。
2) 陈述具体事由,并评论事件,赞扬收信人。
3) 再一次祝贺或表达良好祝愿。

1.2.3 常用词汇(Vocabulary)

congratulate	$v.$ 祝贺
congratulation	$n.$ 祝贺
convey	$v.$ 传达,表达
achievement	$n.$ 成就
effort	$n.$ 努力
be proud of	为……感到自豪
be delighted with	对……感到高兴

1.2.4 套用语句(Useful Expressions)

对具体事情表示祝贺

1) I am much delighted to learn that...
　　很高兴听说……

2) It is a great pleasure to hear of...

得知……,我非常高兴。

3) (My heartfelt) Congratulations to you on...

(衷心地)祝贺你……

4) I would like to offer/convey my warm congratulations to you on...

我要为你的……向你表达热烈的祝贺。

5) Please accept my most sincere congratulations!

请接受我最真诚的祝贺!

评论事件、赞扬收信人

1) This is a special and happy moment for you and I am very proud of your achievement.

对你来说这是一个特别的幸福时刻,我为你的成就感到骄傲。

2) I believe this position will be a new beginning, a chance for you to embrace a fuller life and pave the way for a brilliant future career.

我相信该职位将是你新的开始,也是你拥抱更充实的生活以及步入美好未来的一个机会。

3) My fellow directors and I are delighted that the many years of service you have given to your company have at least been rewarded.

我和所有董事都很高兴,你为公司多年的工作终于得到了回报。

4) For years you have made unremitting efforts in your specialized field and your diligence and intelligence at last win your honor.

你在专业领域里多年的不懈努力,你的勤奋和聪明才智最终使你赢得了该荣誉。

5) I believe as an up and doing person, you will use your head and hands to develop your career to a higher level after the graduation.

我相信,作为一个积极肯干的人,毕业后你将运用头脑和双手使你的事业发展到更高水平。

表达祝愿

1) Best wishes!

最良好的祝愿!

2) All the luck in the world to you!

祝你好运!

3) I wish you luck and success in the coming New Year!

祝来年里好运、成功!

4) I hope you will have nothing but joy and happiness in your life/career.

祝你生活/事业幸福快乐!

1.2.5 写作范例(Samples)

Sample 1

March 10, 2021

Dear Lily,

　　I am much delighted to learn that you have been elected the President of our University English Association. This is a special and happy moment for you and I am very proud of your achievement.

　　The English Association plays an important role in our campus life. Managing such an organization not only is a great challenge to you, but will also enhance your ability comprehensively. I believe this position will be a new beginning, and a chance for you to embrace a fuller life and pave the way for a brilliant future career.

　　Please accept my most sincere congratulations!

Best wishes,
Li Ming

译文

例 1

2021年3月10日

亲爱的莉莉,

　　很高兴听说你当选了我校英语协会会长。对你来说这是一个特别开心的时刻,我为你的成就感到骄傲。

　　英语协会在校园生活中充当重要角色。管理、支持这样的组织对你来说不仅是一个巨大的挑战,同时也会提高你的综合能力。我相信该职位将是你新的开始,也是你拥抱更充实的生活以及步入美好未来的一个机会。

　　请接受我最真挚的祝贺!

祝愿你的,
李明

Sample 2

February 23, 2021

Dear Mr. Smith,

  Congratulations on your promotion to be the sales manager of Shanghai Branch.

  My fellow managers and I are delighted that your work in the marketing field has been recognized this way and we join in sending you our very best wishes for the future.

  Through the three years of working together with you, many of us are well aware of how much you've contributed to the company. We are all looking forward to your trip to Wuhan next month when we will celebrate your advancement in a more formal way.

  Again, congratulations to you, Mr. Smith. May you achieve greater success on your new position as the sales manager of Shanghai Branch!

Sincerely yours,
Yu Bo

译文
例 2

2021年2月23日

亲爱的史密斯先生,

  衷心祝贺你被提升为上海分公司销售经理。

  我和所有经理为你在销售领域的工作获得如此认可感到高兴,同时希望你未来一切都好。

  三年的共事,我们都很了解你对公司所做的巨大贡献。盼望你下月来武汉,这样我们就可以更正式地祝贺你升职了。

  再一次地祝贺你,史密斯先生。祝你在上海分公司销售经理这个岗位上取得更大成就!

你真诚的,
于波

1.2.6 练习(Exercises)

I. Directions: Finish the letter by choosing the proper sentences given.

A. Our best regards to you and your bride once again.

B. She is such a clever and beautiful girl and you two are a perfect match.

C. It was a delightful surprise to hear the news of your upcoming marriage to Miss Alice Black.

D. We beg your acceptance of the enclosed gift as a token of our best wishes.

E. Congratulations!

November 23, 2021

Dear John,

_____
_____
_____
_____
_____

Yours sincerely,

Lily

II. Directions: Fill in the blanks to complete the following letter of congratulations according to the Chinese given.

June 28, 2021

Dear Ellen,

  _____(很高兴听说你将从复旦大学毕业) and get a Master's Degree! Though I cannot go to Shanghai to join in the celebration of your graduation owing to the long distance between the two cities, yet _____(我希望通过此信表达我最诚挚、最热烈的祝福).

  For years you have made unremitting efforts in your specialized field and (你的勤奋和聪明才智使你赢得了最终的荣誉). _____ (我打心底里为你感到高兴和自豪).

  I believe as an up and coming person, you will use your head and hands to develop your career to a higher level after the graduation.

  _____(祝愿你将来取得更大成就).

Yours sincerely,

Li Ming

III. Directions: You are required to write a letter of congratulations according to the information given below.

写信人:王芳
收信人:张东
内容:

　　张东最近被提升为华为公司销售部经理,王芳写信表示祝贺。她认为张东的公司做出了明智的决定,并认为张东在新的工作岗位上会很出色,最后她祝张东取得新成就。

1.3 求职信(Letter of Job Application)

1.3.1 简介(Brief Introduction)

　　求职信是写信人就某一职位向收信人提出请求,是申请信的一种。求职信一般包括以下几个方面的内容:首先要阐述招聘信息来源,以及所申请职位;其次简述个人信息,强调自己的能力,表达抱负,并请求给予面试机会;最后提出自己的希望,希望得到面试的机会,并且告诉对方你的联系方式。

　　求职信的语言属于正式用语,在写作过程中一定要注意用词简洁准确,语气礼貌自信,态度不卑不亢,所给信息具有一定的可信度。尤其是在强调自身经历和优点的时候,更应把握尺度。

　　由于篇幅较短,而申请者需要尽可能地向用人单位推销自己,所以在求职信中宜笼统概说自己的求学和工作经历,突出一至两个吸引眼球的闪光点即可。

1.3.2 写作步骤(Writing Steps)

1) 说明招聘信息的来源,以及所申请的具体职位。
2) 简要自我介绍,展示个人能力、经历及求职动机。
3) 希望给予面试机会并表示感谢。

1.3.3 常用词汇(Vocabulary)

---

apply *v.* 申请
application *n.* 申请
position *n.* 职位
post *n.* 岗位
vacancy *n.* 空位,空缺
graduate *v.* 毕业 *n.* 毕业生
graduation *n.* 毕业

> interview *v./n.* 面试
> résumé *n.* 个人简历
> apply for 申请
> in response to 回答,响应
> job advertisement 招聘广告
> work experience 工作经验
> teamwork spirit 团队精神

1.3.4 套用语句(Useful Expressions)

说明招聘信息来源及求职目的

1) I am writing to apply for the position of...you advertised in yesterday's...
   本人欲申请昨天刊登在……上的……职位。

2) I am writing in response to your advertisement for...
   看到贵公司刊登在……上的广告本人很感兴趣,有意应聘该职位。

3) ...told me that you have a vacancy for...
   ……告诉我,贵单位有个……职位空缺。

自我介绍,展示个人能力

1) To briefly introduce myself, I am a graduate student of...University majoring in...and expect graduation this June.
   简要介绍一下自己,我是……大学……专业今年六月即将毕业的一名学生。

2) Not only have I excellent academic performance in all courses, I also possess the rich experience of...
   我不仅在所有课程中具有优秀的专业表现,而且富有……的经历。

3) The main reason for my confidence in this position lies in...
   我对此职位充满信心的原因在于……

4) My interactive personal skills and teamwork spirit are also appropriate for this post.
   相互配合的技能和团队合作精神使我很适合这个岗位。

5) Please find more details in my enclosed résumé.
   在随信简历中您可以了解本人的详细信息。

请求给予面试机会

1) I look forward to the opportunity of attending an interview.
   我期盼能得到面试的机会。

2) I would be grateful if you could arrange an interview at your earliest convenience.

如能在方便时尽快安排面试，本人将不胜感激。

3) Thank you for your time and patience, and I would greatly appreciate it if you could grant me an interview.

谢谢您的时间和耐心，如能安排面试本人将不胜感激。

1.3.5 写作范例(Samples)

Sample 1

May 24, 2021

Dear Sir,

　　I am writing to apply for the position of sales manager you advertised in yesterday's *China Daily*.

　　To briefly introduce myself, I am a graduate student of Wuhan University majoring in marketing and expect graduation this June. Not only have I excellent academic performance in all courses, I also possess the rich experience of assisting management staff of several renowned international companies, such as Shell and Foxconn. My interactive personal skills and teamwork spirit are also appropriate for this post. For further information, please refer to my attached résumé.

　　I would be grateful if you could arrange an interview at your earliest convenience.

Yours sincerely,
Li Ming

译文

例1

2021年5月24日

尊敬的先生，

　　本人欲申请昨天贵单位刊登在《中国日报》上的销售经理职位。

　　简要介绍一下自己，我是武汉大学市场营销专业今年六月即将毕业的一名学生。我不仅在所有课程中具有优秀的专业表现，而且具有在几家知名国际公司如壳牌、富士康做助理管理员的丰富经历。相互配合的技能和团队合作精神也使我很适合这个岗位。在随信简历中您可以了解本人的详细信息。

　　如能在方便时尽快安排面试，本人将不胜感激。

您真诚的，
李明

Sample 2

June 15, 2021

Dear Sir or Madam,

  In response to your advertisement in the April 10 *Beijing Daily* for a Network Maintenance Engineer, I wish to apply for the position.

  According to the advertisement, your position requires top university, Bachelor or above in Computer Science or equivalent field and proficient in Windows NT 4.0 and LINUX System. I feel that I am competent to meet the requirements. I will be graduating from Graduate School of Tsinghua University this year with a M.S. degree. My studies have included courses in computer control and management and I designed a control simulation system developed with Microsoft Visual InterDev and SQL Server.

  During my education, I have grasped the principals of my major and skills of practice. Not only have I passed CET-6, but more importantly I can communicate with others freely in English. My ability to write and speak English is out of question.

  I would appreciate your time in reviewing my enclosed résumé and if there is any additional information you require, please contact me. I would welcome an opportunity to meet with you for a personal interview.

  With many thanks.

Yours sincerely,
Wang Lin

译文
例 2

2021年6月15日

尊敬的先生或女士，

  看到贵单位刊登在4月10《北京日报》上的招聘网络维护工程师的广告，我特就该职位提出申请。

  据广告描述，该职位要求计算机科学或相关专业熟练掌握 Windows NT 4.0 和 LINUX 系统的本科及以上优秀大学毕业生。我认为自己符合该要求。本人即将从清华大学研究生院毕业并获得硕士学位，学习中包含了计算机控制与管理技术。我曾用微软的 Visual InterDev 和 SQL Server 设计过一个模拟系统。

  学习期间，本人掌握了本专业知识和实践技能。我不仅通过了CET-6考试，而且能够用英语进行自由交流。我的英语口头及笔头表达能力没有问题。

> 如能费时阅读随信所附个人简历，本人将不胜感激。如需了解更多信息，请联系本人。希望能获得面试机会，多谢！
>
> 您真诚的，
> 王林

1.3.6 练习(Exercises)

I. Directions: Finish the letter by choosing the proper sentences given.

A. As you will see from my enclosed résumé, I have been a shorthand typist in the Marketing Department of Enterprise Cables Ltd. for two years.

B. I have been very happy there and have gained a lot of valuable experience.

C. However, the office is quite small and I now wish to broaden my experience and hopefully improve my prospects.

D. Mrs. Phyllis Nash, your Personnel Officer has told me that you have a vacancy for a Marketing Assistant.

E. I am able to attend and interview at any time and hope to hear from you soon.

F. I would like to be considered for this post.

G. My present employer has written the enclosed reference and has kindly agreed to give further details if you are interested in my application.

June 23, 2021

Dear Mr. Barker,

_____
_____
_____
_____
_____
_____
_____
_____

Yours sincerely,
Jean Carson

II. Directions: Fill in the blanks to complete the following letter of application according to the Chinese given.

June 22, 2021

Dear Sir,

　　_____ (看到广告,我很感兴趣) a Sales Manager in yesterday's *China Daily* and _____ (希望您能考虑让我担任这一职位).

　　_____ (我的基本情况都在所附简历中), from which you will see that I_____ (有 12 年的工作经验) in the sales department of two well-known companies. I thoroughly enjoy my work and am very happy in Phoenix Plastic Ltd., but feel that the time has come when my experience in marketing has prepared me for the responsibility of full sales management.

　　_____ (如果需要的话,本人将很乐意为您提供个人更详细的资料) and I look forward to hearing from you.

Yours faithfully,
Li Ming

III. Directions: You are required to write a letter of application according to the information given below.

　　李强在美国修完了一门商业管理课程,欲申请一份行政管理人员工作。他曾在美国几家工商企业担任过多种不同的职务,获得了较丰富的商务和办公管理知识。请以李强的名义写一封求职信。

1.4 投诉信(Letter of Complaint)

1.4.1 简介(Brief Introduction)

　　日常生活中,人们常会因各种问题写信向有关部门投诉,以求问题得到解决;商务交往中,产品和服务不令人满意是常有的事,如果遇到,可以写信向相关单位投诉,以实现退换或索赔等愿望。

　　写投诉信时要客气,但语气要坚定;另外投诉的内容要具体,要明确指出问题出在哪儿以及你的具体要求;要证明责任确实在对方;最后还可加上由此给你来的不便或伤害,以加强投诉信的分量。再者,如需要索赔,须注意:索赔具有时效性,即必须在合同规定的有效期内(通常是货到后30天内)提出索赔,否则,违约方可以不予受理。

1.4.2 写作步骤(Writing Steps)

1) 向对方投诉并表示遗憾。
2) 叙述事情的前因后果和造成的不便及损失。
3) 提出处理意见或敦促对方采取措施,比如赔礼道歉、退货、退款等。
4) 结尾客套语。

1.4.3 常用词汇(Vocabulary)

```
complain     v. 投诉,抱怨
complaint    n. 投诉,抱怨
delivery     n. 递送,交付
shortage     n. 短缺
delay        v./n. 延期
damage       v./n. 破损
claim        v./n. 索赔
replace      v. 更换
replacement  n. 更换
refund       v./n. 退款
repair       v./n. 维修
```

1.4.4 套用语句(Useful Expressions)

投诉并表示遗憾

1) I am writing to complain about...
   此信是要对……进行投诉。
2) I am sorry to trouble you but I am afraid that I have to make a serious complaint.
   很抱歉打扰您,但我必须郑重提出投诉。
3) I really hate to complain, but one thing is really disturbing me.
   我真的讨厌投诉,但最近有一件事情确实令人烦心。
4) I am sorry to tell you that there should be cause to complain about...
   我很遗憾地告诉你有关投诉……的事由。

投诉事由

1) The goods certainly do not match the samples and are unsuited to the needs of...

货物显然与样品不符,并且不能满足……的要求。

2) The quality of...was not up to our expectations.

……的质量未能达到我方期望。

3) Upon examination, we found you have evidently sent us the wrong goods.

经检查,我们发现贵方明显发错了货。

4) We regret to report that some of the goods are badly damaged when delivered on...

我们抱歉地通知贵方,……交付时,部分货物已严重损坏。

5) There is a shortage in the shipment of...which we received from you this morning.

我方今天上午收到由贵方运来的……有短缺。

6) We regret to have to protest about the late delivery of...ordered on July 2.

我们很抱歉不得不对7月2日订购的……被延迟送货提出抗议。

提出批评及处理意见或敦促对方采取措施

1) We know that you are not generally careless, but we would like your assurance that this will not happen again.

我们深知你们并不经常出错,但我们希望能确保这类差错不再发生。

2) We have no choice but to return them to you and require a replacement of the quantity ordered.

我方别无选择,只能退回货物,并要求全数更换。

3) We ask you, therefore, to ship...by airmail immediately on receipt of this letter.

因此,请贵方收到此信后立刻空运……

4) We need to have...either repaired or replaced and the shipping cost reimbursed.

我方需要将……修理或更换,并要求补偿运费。

5) We hereby bring up/make/raise a formal claim with you for the sum of...in all.

我方特此正式提出总金额为……的索赔要求。

6) We put in a claim for damage/inferior quality.

我方要求对破损和劣质物质进行赔偿。

结尾客套语

1) Thank you for your consideration. And I am looking forward to an early reply.

谢谢您的考虑。期待您尽快回复。

2) I would be very grateful if you could look into the matter as soon as possible. And I am looking forward to an early reply.

如果您能尽快调查此事,我将不胜感激。期待您尽快回复。

1.4.5 写作范例(Samples)

Sample 1

> February 13, 2021
>
> Dear Sir/Madam,
>
>   I am writing to complain about the Hero fountain pen I have bought from your shop recently. The problem is that I have been unable to use the pen because it leaks and never writes without making blots. I am very disappointed with my purchase.
>
>   On the advice of the manager of your store, I am returning the pen to you and enclosing it with this letter for correction of the fault.
>
>   Would you please let me know whether you would be willing to replace it with a new one and send it to me as soon as possible?
>
>   Thank you for your consideration. And I am looking forward to an early reply.
>
> Sincerely yours,
Li Ming

译文
例1

> 2021年2月13日
>
> 尊敬的先生/女士,
>
>   此信是要对本人最近在贵店所买的"英雄"牌自来水笔进行投诉。问题是,此笔漏墨水,每次使用都弄得墨迹斑斑。我对此非常失望。
>
>   根据贵店经理的建议,我先将此笔退回给您,并附上此信,希望问题能够解决。
>
>   不知贵方是否愿意更换一只新笔并尽快寄给我?
>
>   谢谢您的考虑。期待您尽快回复。
>
> 您真诚的,
李明

Sample 2

> May 20, 2021
>
> Dear Sir/Madam,
>
>   I am sorry to trouble you but I am afraid that I have to make a serious complaint.

Today we have received your bill for 150 name-bearing crystal vases which you sent us the other day. We had ordered these vases on condition that they should reach us by the end of February. But they arrived here 15 days behind the schedule.

The customers refused to accept the goods because they arrived too late. Since the vases bear their names, we cannot sell them to other customers. So we asked the customers again and again to take the vases, and finally they agreed to accept them, but at a price cut of 30%.

You may understand how we have lost the customer's confidence in us. In this situation, we have to ask you to compensate for the loss we have suffered. We are looking forward to hearing from you soon.

Yours faithfully,
Zhang Dong

译文

例 2

2021年5月20日

尊敬的先生或女士，

很抱歉打扰您，但我必须郑重提出投诉。

今天我们收到了前几天贵方送来刻有名字的150个水晶花瓶的账单。我们订购这批花瓶的前提是必须在二月底到货，但是却迟到了15天。

因为到货太晚，顾客拒绝接收这批货物。花瓶上刻有顾客的名字，因此我们不能卖给其他客人。在我们再三请求下，顾客终于答应接收这批花瓶，但是砍价30%。

贵方可以理解我们是如何失去客户对我们的信心的。在这种情形下，我方要求贵方赔偿我们所遭受的损失。盼尽快回复！

您真诚的，
张东

1.4.6 练习(Exercises)

I. Directions: Finish the letter by choosing the proper sentences given.

A. Unfortunately, the shoes just arrived today about 16 days late.

B. We trust that there will be no repetition of this problem.

C. You might remember that on April 20 we placed an order with you for 50 pairs of sports shoes, emphasizing at the time that the ordered shoes should be delivered before May 20.

D. This delay has put us in a very difficult position.

E. I really hate to complain, but one thing is really disturbing me.

July 4, 2021

Dear Sir,

_____
_____
_____
_____
_____

Yours truly,
Wang Fan

II. Directions: Fill in the blanks to complete the following letter of complaint according to the Chinese given.

December 23, 2021

Dear Sir or Madam,

_____ (此信是为了向您投诉本人上个月在广州出差时在您商店里买的照相机). There I took some pictures, yet, when I had it developed after I got home, I found no pictures printed at all. I feel very frustrated about it.
_____ (我已将相机寄回贵商店,并坚决要求退款).

Yours sincerely,
Wang Lan

III. Directions: You are required to write a letter of complaint according to the information given below.

As a student, you write a letter to your University President complaining about the bad canteen food and service on campus.

1.5 道歉信(Letter of Apology)

1.5.1 简介(Brief Introduction)

因过失或疏忽做错了事,给别人带来麻烦或损失,要立即写信给对方赔礼道歉,这是一种礼貌。道歉信主要是向收信人表明歉意,请求对方谅解自己的过失。写道歉信时要注意,不是找借口为自己辩护,而是要承认自己的过错,并提出弥补过错的具体建议和方法。道歉信应语气诚恳,用词准确,内容直截了当。

1.5.2 写作步骤(Writing Steps)

1) 表示歉意。
2) 说明道歉的具体原因。
3) 提出补救建议。
4) 再次道歉,请求谅解。

1.5.3 常用词汇(Vocabulary)

apologize	*v.*	道歉
apology	*n.*	道歉
deepest	*adj.*	最深的
appointment	*n.*	约会,约定
extremely	*adv.*	极其,非常
cancel	*v.*	取消
promptly	*adv.*	迅速,立即
inconvenience	*n.*	不便,麻烦

1.5.4 套用语句(Useful Expressions)

表示歉意

1) I am writing this letter to apologize for...
   我写这封信是为了……向您道歉。
2) I would like to give you my apology for...

对于……我向你道歉。

3) Here is my deepest apology for forgetting the appointment we had made.

我把约会给忘了,对此深表歉意。

4) I'm extremely sorry that I had to cancel our appointment yesterday.

非常抱歉取消了昨天的约会。

5) Sorry for not answering promptly.

很抱歉没有及时回复。

再次道歉,请求谅解

1) Once again, I'm sorry for causing all the inconvenience./I apologize for any inconvenience this may have caused you.

再一次,我为所有的不便表示歉意。

2) I sincerely hope that you can accept my apologies.

真心希望你能接受我的道歉。

3) Please allow me to say sorry again.

请允许我再次表示歉意。

1.5.5 写作范例(Samples)

Sample 1

November 3, 2020

Dear Mr. Wilson,

　　I would like to express my apologies for not being able to keep our scheduled appointment last Friday.

　　I attempted to send a message to you that my car broke down on my way to your office and I needed to immediately deal with towing and subsequent repairs. I hope you have received my message. I will call your office within this week to reschedule another appointment that is convenient for you. I look forward to meeting you.

　　Once again, I apologize for any inconvenience this may have caused

Yours sincerely,

Li Xiao

译文
例 1

2020 年 11 月 3 日

亲爱的威尔逊先生，

　　十分抱歉上周五我没能赴约。

　　在前往您办公室的途中，我的车抛锚了，我必须马上应付拖车以及随后的维修问题。我曾给您发去信息通知您，希望您已经收到了我的信息。我会在这个星期之内打电话到您办公室，重新预约一个您方便的时间。期待与您会面。

　　再一次，我为所有的不便表示歉意。

您真诚的，
李啸

Sample 2

January 11, 2021

Dear Linda,

　　I am terribly sorry to tell you that I have lost the book *Pride and Prejudice* that you were so kind to lend me last month.

　　I had finished it and intended to return it to you today. However, when I came to my room last night, it was nowhere to be found. Maybe someone has taken it away without first letting me know. I am still trying to get back the book. If I fail to find it, I will buy a new one for you.

　　I sincerely hope that you can accept my apologies.

Yours truly,
Frank

译文
例 2

2021 年 1 月 11 日

亲爱的琳达，

　　非常抱歉我遗失了你上个月借给我的《傲慢与偏见》。

　　我已经读完了这本书，并且准备今天把它还给你。可是当我昨晚回房间的时候，我哪儿都找不到它。也许是有人没跟我打招呼就把它拿去看了。我仍然在努力找回这本书。

> 如果还找不到，我就买一本新的给你。
>   真诚地希望你能够接受我的道歉。
>
> 　　　　　　　　　　　　　　　　　　　　你真诚的，
> 　　　　　　　　　　　　　　　　　　　　弗兰克

1.5.6 练习(Exercises)

I. Directions: Put the following parts into proper order to make a complete letter of apology.

A. I hope you will not leave the city this week, and I will call on you this Friday afternoon at three o'clock.

B. Please wait for me in your hotel at the appointed time.

C. I am very sorry that I was out when you came to see me yesterday morning.

D. Had that not happened, naturally I would have been with you.

E. Once again, I sincerely hope you could understand me and accept my apology.

F. However, my father suddenly had a heart attack, and I had to take him to the hospital in a hurry.

G. I had told you that I would be available that morning.

> Dear Jasmine,
>
> _____
> _____
> _____
> _____
> _____
> _____
> _____
>
> 　　　　　　　　　　　　　　　　　　　　Yours,
> 　　　　　　　　　　　　　　　　　　　　Chris

II. Directions: Fill in the blanks to complete the following letter of apology according to the Chinese given.

February 17, 2021

Dear Mr. Winston,

_____(十分抱歉)for the mix-up on your last order. We recently _____(雇用了一名新的销售人员)who was not familiar with your systems. We have _____(更正了您的订单并发货)this morning. We have applied a 10% discount on your order, and again _____(抱歉给您带来了不便).

Yours sincerely,
Paul Cordero
Customer Service Manager

III. Directions: You are required to write a letter of apology according to the information given below.

假设你叫李明。由于你无法到机场去接朋友汤姆,请给他写一封道歉信。要点如下:
1) 为无法到机场接机表示歉意。
2) 说明原因:昨天接到通知要参加重要的商务会议,并要在会议上发言,会议上午11点才结束,比接机时间晚了2小时。
3) 会议结束后会立刻到酒店和汤姆见面。
4) 再次道歉。

1.6 邀请信(Letter of Invitation)

1.6.1 简介(Brief Introduction)

邀请信分为两种:一种是个人信函,例如邀请某人共进晚餐、参加宴会、观看电影等;另一种是事务信函,一般是邀请参加会议、学术活动等。第一种邀请信邀请的对象一般是朋友、熟人,所以内容、格式上的要求都比较宽松,只要表明邀请意图,说明活动的内容、时间、地点等即可。第二种邀请信一般由会议或学术活动组委会的某一个负责人来写,以组委会的名义发出,这类邀请信的措辞要相对正式一些,语气要热情有礼。

1.6.2 写作步骤(Writing Steps)

1) 表明邀请意图以及活动的名称、时间、地点。
2) 说明活动的相关事宜,表达希望对方能够参加的诚意。
3) 请收信人对发出的邀请做出反馈。

1.6.3 常用词汇(Vocabulary)

```
opportunity   n. 机会,时机
invite        v. 邀请,招待
invitation    n. 邀请
attend        v. 出席
expect        v. 期待,等待
presence      n. 出席,参加
confirm       v. 确认,确定
participate   v. 参加,参与
```

1.6.4 套用语句(Useful Expressions)

发出邀请

1) May I take the opportunity to invite you to...?
   我能借此机会邀请您……吗?

2) It gives me the greatest pleasure to invite you to...
   能邀请您……是我最大的荣幸。

3) We sincerely hope you can attend...
   我们衷心希望您能来参加……

4) We are expecting with great pleasure to see you.
   我们怀着愉快的心情期待着与你相见。

5) We hope you can come and look forward to seeing you.
   我们希望你能来并期待着与你见面。

6) Request the honor of your presence.
   敬请您出席。

请对方回复

1) Please let me know as soon as possible if you can come.
   请尽快告知你是否能来。

2) Please confirm your participation at your earliest convenience.
   请您在方便的时候尽快通知我们是否出席。

3) R. S. V. P./Please reply.
   敬请回复

1.6.5 写作范例(Samples)

Sample 1
(Personal Letter of Invitation)

> Dear Brian,
>
> I know you are interested in antiques, so I'm sure you'll be interested in Mr. and Mrs. Clark! They are coming here to supper next Saturday night, October the twelfth, and we'd like you and Rose to come, too.
>
> Mr. and Mrs. Clark are very charming couple we met in Chicago last summer. They have a wonderful collection of antiques. I'm sure you and Rose will thoroughly enjoy the evening in their company.
>
> We're planning supper at seven, and we are expecting with great pleasure to see you both.
>
> Affectionately yours,
>
> Barbara

译文
例 1
(个人邀请信)

> 亲爱的布莱恩,
>
> 我知道你对古董很感兴趣,所以我确信你也会对克拉克夫妇感兴趣！下周六晚上,也就是十月十二日,他们会到我家来吃晚餐,希望你和露丝也能来。
>
> 克拉克先生和太太是我们去年夏天在芝加哥遇到的一对很可爱的夫妇。他们有许多很棒的古董收藏品。我相信在他们的陪伴下,你和露丝会度过一个十分愉快的夜晚。
>
> 晚餐计划在七点开始。我们怀着愉快的心情期待与你们俩见面。
>
> 爱你的,
>
> 芭芭拉

Sample 2
(Business Letter of Invitation)

> October 5, 2021
>
> Dear Sir or Madam,
>
> On behalf of the Secretariat of Environment Forum, I would like to extend a special

invitation to you and your organization to participate in the upcoming Wuhan International Environment Forum to be held in Wuhan, China, 21-23 October, 2021.

This year's forum will discuss the issues of environmental protection and responsibilities our society shall bear. We sincerely hope you will join us in the Forum to share your perspectives and experiences.

If you can accept the invitation, please let us know as soon as possible so that we can prepare the final program. We eagerly look forward to your kind reply.

Secretariat
Wuhan International Environment Forum

译文
例2
(事务邀请信)

2021年10月5日

亲爱的先生或女士,

我谨代表环境论坛秘书处,特别邀请您和您的机构组织参加即将开幕的武汉国际环境论坛。这次论坛将于2021年10月21日至23日在中国武汉举行。

今年的论坛将讨论环境保护以及我们的社会应该承担的责任问题。衷心希望您能够参加这次论坛,和我们分享您的观点和体会。

如果您接受邀请,请尽快告知,以便我们安排最终的议程。热切期待您的回复。

秘书处
武汉国际环境论坛

1.6.6 练习(Exercises)

I. Directions: Put the following parts into proper order to make a complete letter of invitation.

A. Since you are an internationally acclaimed scholar in this field, your participation will be among the highlights of the conference.

B. The conference is to be held in Shanghai, China, from August 10 to August 13, 2021.

C. You will receive further details later, but we would appreciate having your acceptance soon so we may complete our agenda.

D. On behalf of the CHI Computer Society, I would be very pleased to invite you to attend and chair a session of the forthcoming conference on Information Technology.

E. We sincerely hope you could accept our invitation.

Dear Professor Scott,

_____
_____
_____
_____
_____
_____
_____
_____
_____
_____

Sincerely yours,
Zhang Hua

II. Directions: Fill in the blanks to complete the following letter of invitation according to the Chinese given.

March 17, 2021

Dear Mr. and Mrs. Taylor,

  As the parents of the bride, I would like to _____
_____(借此机会邀请你们参加我女儿的婚礼), Sandra Green to her fiancé Adam Locke. On this joyous occasion, we wish to _____
_____(与最亲密的朋友和家人共度这一天).

  The formal event will be located at the Fire Lake Country Club on the fifteenth of August at three o'clock, two thousand and nine.

  _____(敬请回复)by the fifteenth of June to _____
_____(确认是否参加). _____(我们希望能在那儿与你们见面) to enjoy this special day with friends and family.

Sincerely Yours,
Margaret Green

III. Directions: You are required to write a letter of invitation according to the information given below.

假设你是英语系的一名助理,名叫王海。你准备代表英语系邀请著名学者 Mr. Anderson 于 4 月 11 日(星期六)来学院讲学,题目是《英国文学》。请写一封邀请信。

1.7 询价信(Letter of Inquiry)

1.7.1 简介(Brief Introduction)

在贸易中,要达成一笔交易需经过反复磋商,即买卖双方通过函电或其他方式相互洽谈、沟通、交换意见,从而达成一致。询价信用于交易时买方向卖方询问和了解商品的价格、货色、付款方式、交货期限等销售条件。写作询价信时,语言表达要准确、具体、简洁。

1.7.2 写作步骤(Writing Steps)

1) 告知获得对方商品信息的来源以及写此函的目的。
2) 请对方提供详细的产品目录、价格表、样品等。
3) 有时可说明询价方的公司业务范围、规模和商品销售前景等。
4) 提出要求,盼望早日回复。

1.7.3 常用词汇(Vocabulary)

```
inquiry        n. 询问,质询
manufacturer   n. 制造商,制造厂
catalogue      n. 目录,一览表
brochure       n. 手册,小册子
quote          v. 报价
discount       n. 折扣
term           n. 条款
payment        n. 支付,付款
competitive    adj. 竞争的,(价格等)有竞争力的
sample         n. 样品,样本
material       n. 材料,原料
purchase       v./n. 购买
```

1.7.4 套用语句(Useful Expressions)

信息来源

1) We have heard that your company has put a new product on the market.
   我们听说贵公司刚刚在市场上推出了一款新产品。
2) We have seen your ad in the newspaper, and we are interested in your products.
   我们在报纸上看到了你们的广告,并且对你们的产品很感兴趣。
3) As we have learned from…, you are the manufacturer of…
   我们从……得知,贵方是……的生产商。

请对方提供详细情况

1) Please send us your latest catalogue/price list/brochure/…
   请给我们寄来您最新的目录/价格清单/商品手册/……
2) Kindly quote us your lowest price for…
   请报给我们你方关于……的最低价格。
3) We should appreciate further details/information about your…
   希望贵方能为我们提供……的详细信息。
4) Will you let us know what discount you give for large quantities?
   如果大量购买可以享受什么折扣?
5) When quoting, please state your terms of payment and the discounts you allow.
   报价时,请说明付款方式以及贵方允许的折扣。

提出要求

1) If your quality is good and the price is reasonable, we will place a large order with you.
   如果贵方产品质量良好,价格合理,我们将大量订购。
2) We ask you to make every effort to quote at competitive prices in order to secure our business.
   为了保证我们的交易,请尽量给出具有竞争力的报价。

1.7.5 写作范例(Samples)

Sample 1

March 3, 2021

Dear Sir,

　　We have learned from *China Daily* that you manufacture a range of handbags.

　　Would you please send us a copy of your handbag catalogue with details of your prices and terms of payment? We would be obliged if you could also supply samples of the different qualities of material used.

We operate a quality retail business and if you supply goods of the quality required, we may place regular orders with you. Looking forward to your early reply.

Yours faithfully,
Albert Jones
Purchasing Manager

译文
例 1

2021年3月3日

亲爱的先生,

我们从《中国日报》上了解到贵方生产各种手提包。

能否请贵方给我方寄来一份手提包产品目录,包括价格和付款方式的详细信息？如能提供所使用的不同材料的样品,我们将不胜感激。

我方是经营高品质产品的零售商,如果贵方提供的产品质量符合要求,我方会定期下订单。期待贵方早日回复。

您忠实的,
艾伯特·琼斯
采购经理

Sample 2

January 15, 2021

Dear Sir or Madam,

Sunrise Trading Co., Ltd. has informed us that you are an exporter of all cotton bedsheets. Would you please send us the details of your various ranges, including sizes, colors, prices, and some samples?

We are a large dealer in textiles and believe there is a promising market in our area for moderately priced goods of this kind mentioned.

When quoting, please state your terms of payment and the discounts you would allow on purchases of quantities of not less than 100 dozen of individual items. Looking forward to your prompt reply.

Yours faithfully,
David Brown
Purchasing Manager

译文
例 2

> 2021年1月15日
>
> 亲爱的先生或女士，
>
> 　　我们通过日出贸易有限公司了解到，贵方是全棉床单出口商。能请贵方将产品各种系列的详细信息，包括尺寸、颜色、价格以及样品寄给我方吗？
>
> 　　我方是纺织品行业的大型销售商。我们相信，价格适中的这类产品在本地市场有很好的销售前景。
>
> 　　报价时，请告知贵方的付款条件，以及购买100打以上的产品贵方所能给出的折扣。期待您及时回复。
>
> 　　　　　　　　　　　　　　　　　　　　　　　　您忠实的，
> 　　　　　　　　　　　　　　　　　　　　　　　　大卫·布朗
> 　　　　　　　　　　　　　　　　　　　　　　　　采购经理

1.7.6 练习(Exercises)

I. Directions: Put the following parts into proper order to make a complete letter of inquiry.

A. Please send us a catalog and price list of your products.

B. We used to purchase these products from other sources.

C. We have seen your advertisement online which aroused our great interest in your sportswear.

D. Thank you for your assistance and we are looking forward to your early reply.

E. We may now prefer to buy from your company because we understand that you are able to supply larger quantities at more attractive prices.

F. It would also be appreciated if you could include your terms of payment and inform us how soon you can arrange for shipment upon receipt of our order.

Dear Sales Manager,

_____
_____
_____
_____
_____
_____
_____

>   Yours sincerely,
>   Michael Smith
>   Purchasing Manager

II. Directions: Fill in the blanks to complete the following letter of inquiry according to the Chinese given.

> Dear Sir,
> _____（今天我们收到了贵方寄来的促销信件和产品手册）. We believe that you would do well here in the U.S.A. Kindly send us _____（更详细的产品价格和销售条件）. We ask you to _____（尽量给出具有竞争力的报价）in order to secure our business. _____（期待您尽快回复）.
>   Yours sincerely,
>   Alex Grey

III. Directions: You are required to write a letter of inquiry according to the information given below.

假定你是某公司的采购部经理。你在杂志上看到一家丝绸服装公司的产品广告,十分感兴趣,希望建立贸易联系。请写一封询价信,了解对方的产品及其价格、付款条件和折扣等。

1.8 报价信(Letter of Quotation)

1.8.1 简介(Brief Introduction)

报价信用于交易时卖方答复买方在询价信中对商品情况的询问。报价分为报实盘和报虚盘。虚盘不规定有效日期,并附有保留条件,无约束力;实盘则相反,一旦报盘被接受,就不能撤盘。无论是询价信还是报价信,语言表达均要准确、具体、切题,切忌模棱两可。

1.8.2 写作步骤(Writing Steps)

1) 感谢对方的询问。

2) 针对对方询问的内容给出答复。

3) 做出保证,表达与对方合作的愿望。

1.8.3 常用词汇(Vocabulary)

quotation	*n.* 报价
enclose	*v.* 把……装入信封,附入
offer	*v./n.* 出价,报价
compare	*v.* 比较,相比
favorably	*adv.* 有利地
competitor	*n.* 竞争者,对手
assure	*v.* 保证,担保
order	*v./n.* 订购,订单
requirement	*n.* 要求,必要条件

1.8.4 套用语句(Useful Expressions)

感谢对方的询问

1) We thank you for your inquiry of July 10 for...
   感谢贵方7月10日对……的询价。

2) We welcome your inquiry, and thanks for your interest in our products.
   欢迎您的询价,感谢您对我们的产品感兴趣。

提供报价

1) We are pleased to enclose our price list and terms of payment for your consideration.
   很荣幸地为您附上我们的价格清单和付款条件供您考虑。

2) In reply to your inquiry of May 7, we have pleasure in making the following offer...
   针对贵方5月7日的询价,我方十分乐意提供如下报价……

3) Enclosed you will find details of our conditions of sales and terms of payment.
   随信附有我方的具体销售条件和付款条件。

4) Our prices compare favorably with those of our competitors.
   我们的价格与其他竞争对手相比是十分优惠的。

5) A ...% discount is offered on payment within a few weeks.

几周之内付款可以享受……的折扣。

做出保证,盼望合作

1) We can assure you that your order will be dealt with promptly.

我们保证会迅速处理贵方的订单。

2) We are sure that these goods will meet your requirements, and we look forward to your early order.

我们确信这些货品能满足您的需求,期待您早日订货。

1.8.5 写作范例(Samples)

Sample 1

March 6, 2021

Dear sir,

We welcome your inquiry, and thanks for your interest in our handbags.

We are pleased to enclose a copy of our latest catalogue, together with samples of some materials we regularly use in the manufacture of our products.

Our sales representative for the United States will be in Washington next month, and we have asked him to call on you. He will bring a wide range of our products and is authorized to discuss the terms of an order with you.

We are sure that our product materials and workmanship will meet your requirements, and we look forward to receiving your order soon.

Yours sincerely,
Bill Douglas
Sales Manager

译文

例1

2021年3月6日

亲爱的先生,

欢迎贵方的询价,感谢贵方对我方生产的手提包感兴趣。

很荣幸地为贵方附上一份最新的产品目录,以及我方通常用来制作产品的一些材料样品。

我方驻美国的销售代表下个月将会前往华盛顿。我们已经通知他去拜访贵方。他会带上我方生产的多种产品,并且我方已经授权他去和贵方协商订单条款。

相信我方产品的用料和工艺一定能满足贵方的需求。期待早日收到贵方的订单。

您真诚的,
比尔·道格拉斯
销售经理

Sample 2

January 18, 2021

Dear Sir,

We are very pleased to receive your inquiry of Jan. 15 and enclose our illustrated catalog and price list giving the details you ask for. Also by separate post, we are sending you some samples and feel confident that when you have examined them you will agree the goods are both excellent in quality and reasonable in price.

Regard to purchases in quantities of not less than 100 dozen of individual items, we would allow you a discount of 3%.

Because of their softness and durability, our all cotton bed-sheets are rapidly becoming popular. After studying our prices you will not be surprised to learn that it is difficult to meet the demand. But if you place your order before the end of this month, we would ensure prompt shipment. Looking forward to your early reply.

Yours faithfully,
Yuan Jun
Sales Manager

译文
例 2

2021年1月18日

亲爱的先生,

非常高兴收到贵方1月15日的询价信,随信附上我方带有插图的产品目录以及价格单,为贵方提供所需的详细信息。另外,我方用一份单独的邮件给贵方寄去了几件样品。我们很有信心,当贵方查看了这些样品后一定会认同,我方产品质优价廉。

至于购买超过100打以上的产品,我方可以给出3%的折扣。

我方生产的全棉床单质地柔软,经久耐用,迅速受到消费者的欢迎。在贵方研究了我

方价格之后,对于我方产品供不应求这一点,贵方一定不会感到惊讶。但是如果贵方能够在本月底之前下订单,我方可以确保立刻发货。期待您尽快回复。

您忠实的,
袁俊
销售经理

1.8.6 练习(Exercises)

I. Directions: Put the following parts into proper order to make a complete letter of quotation.

A. It gives us great pleasure to send along the technical information on the model together with the catalogue and price list.

B. But if you place your order within the next ten days, we make you a firm offer of delivery by the end of December.

C. There is a heavy demand for our products which we are finding it difficult to meet.

D. We look forward to the opportunity of cooperating with you.

E. Thank you for your inquiry of Dec. 15 concerning our company's laptop computers (Model AS100).

Dear Sir,

_____
_____
_____
_____
_____
_____
_____
_____

Sincerely yours,
William Roberts
Manager

II. Directions: Fill in the blanks to complete the following letter of quotation according to the Chinese given.

November 24, 2020

Dear Sir,

_____(感谢贵方11月22日的询价). In compliance with your request, _____(我们随信寄去了一份报价单)for velvet curtains No. 21 and 22. _____(至于相关的样品), we have dispatched them to you by separate airmail.

  Our velvet curtains _____(质量良好,价格适中). As our stocks are low and the demand is heavy, _____(希望贵方能够尽快下订单).

  Awaiting your esteemed favors and orders.

Yours faithfully,
Han Hui
Sales Manager

III. Directions: You are required to write a letter of quotation according to the information given below.

  假定你是一家丝绸服装公司的销售经理,收到某公司9月19日的询价信。请写一封报价信,内容如下:感谢对方对本公司的产品感兴趣;随信附上交易条款,包括价格清单和折扣;另寄去样品;希望产品能满足对方需求,期待与对方合作。

1.9 订购信(Letter of Placing an Order)

1.9.1 简介(Brief Introduction)

  订购信一般用于订购某种货物或机票、车票,属于商务信函。在书写订购信的时候,最重要的是要清楚明白地说明所要订购的数量、价格、规格等,如果是机票、车票等,则须说明出发地、目的地、出发时间等。此外,写明自己的名字、地址、邮编,以及所期望的送货、付款方式等也是非常重要的。要避免写冗长的句子,因为此类信函以传达信息为主,所以让对方明白意图是最重要的。

1.9.2 写作步骤(Writing Steps)

1) 感谢对方提供报价和其他信息。
2) 订购具体事宜(包括:产品名称、尺寸、颜色、型号、目录号、订单号、数量、单价、包装方式、装运条件、交货、付款方式等）。
3）就订单相关事宜向对方提出要求。
4）说明随信所附文件等。

1.9.3 常用词汇（Vocabulary）

provide that	假如，只要
discount	$n.$ 折扣
look forward to	期待
purchasing department	采购部
Co. Ltd	有限责任公司
as per	根据
order sheet	订单

1.9.4 套用语句（Useful Expressions）

感谢对方提供报价和其他信息

1）We thank you for your quotation of...
　　感谢贵方对……的报价。
2）We thank you for your letter about...
　　感谢贵方关于……的来信。

订购货物

1）We are pleased to place an order with you for...
　　我们很高兴向贵方订购……
2）We have the pleasure of/in handing/sending an order for...
　　我们很高兴发给／寄给贵方一份……的订单。
3）I want to order...to be delivered to...
　　我想订购……，货送到……

就订单相关事宜向对方提出要求

1）Provided that it will be delivered on time/within...days.
　　条件是贵方能准时／在……天内送货。
2）We trust you will be able to meet our need in this respect.
　　希望贵公司能够在这方面满足我方的需要。
3）Hoping that our order will get your prompt response.

希望我方的订单能够得到迅速处理。

4) We hope that the packing and delivery will be careful.

我们希望货物能仔细包装,小心运送。

5) Your immediate reply will be appreciated.

贵方若能立即处理该订单,我方将十分感谢。

1.9.5 写作范例(Samples)

Sample 1

<pre>
                                                          May 20, 2021
Dear Sir,
    We thank you for your letter of May 15 about English dictionaries and are pleased to
place an order with you for 2,000 copies provided that it will be delivered within 20 days
from the day you receive our order and you will give us a 10% discount.
    We trust you will be able to meet our need in these respects, and we look forward to
placing further orders with you.

                                                          Yours faithfully,
                                                          (Signature)
                                                          F. George
                                                          Purchasing Department
                                                          ABC Co. Ltd
</pre>

译文

例 1

<pre>
                                                          2021年5月20日
亲爱的先生,
    感谢贵公司在5月15日的来信中提供关于英语词典的信息,很高兴向贵公司订购
2000本词典,条件是贵方能在收到订单后20天之内将货送到,并给我方10%的折扣。
    希望贵公司能够在这方面满足我方需要,并期望能进一步与贵公司合作。

                                                          您忠实的,
                                                          (签名)
                                                          F. 乔治
                                                          采购部
                                                          ABC有限责任公司
</pre>

Sample 2

August 27, 2021

Dear Sir,

 We thank you for your quotation of your Aug. 23 letter about the small Christmas gifts. Now we have the pleasure of sending you an order for various items as per our Order Sheet No. 1345.

 We hope that the packing and delivery will be careful.

 Your immediate reply will be appreciated.

 Enclosed please find our Order Sheet No. 1345.

Sincerely yours,
(Signature)
C. Golf

译文
例 2

2021年8月27日

亲爱的先生,

 感谢贵公司在8月23日的来信中向我方提供关于圣诞小礼物的报价,很高兴随函附上我方所需各类货物的订单一份,订单号为:1345。

 我们希望货物能仔细包装,小心运送。

 贵方若能立即处理该订单,我方将十分感谢。

 随信附上1345号订单。

您真诚的,
(签名)
C. 高夫

1.9.6 练习(Exercises)

I. Directions: Finish the letter by choosing the proper sentences given.

A. Provided that the price will remain unchanged.

B. Enclosed please find our Order Sheet No. 1324.

C. We thank you for your letter of June 17 and are pleased to place an order with you as per our Order Sheet No. 1324.

June 22, 2021

Dear Mr. John Smith,

_____
_____
_____
_____
_____

                        Yours faithfully,
                        （Signature）
                        Ding Zhiwen
                        Purchasing Manager
                        Cindy Garment Co.

II. Directions: Fill in the blanks to complete the following letter placing an order according to the Chinese given.

Dear Mr. Li,

_____（感谢贵公司在 7 月 13 日对激光打印机的报价）. We are so interested in your products. _____（我方决定向贵公司订购 15 台型号为 MP983 的激光打印机）, provided that _____（贵公司需要提供售后服务）. Enclosed please find _____（$22500 支票一张）.
Please give us reply as soon as you receive our letter.

                        Yours Sincerely,
                        John Smith

III. Directions: You are required to write a letter placing an order according to the information given below.

1) 收到来信，表示感谢。
2) 表示对新型 AW－501 录音机感兴趣。
3) 拟购 10 台录音机，询问价格可否降低(cut down the price)。
4) 拟于二十六日前往贵公司看货。

1.10 推荐信(Letter of Recommendation)

1.10.1 简介(Brief Introduction)

推荐信是一个人为推荐另一个人去接受某个职位或参与某项工作而写的信件,是一种应用写作文体。推荐信应多写被推荐人的优点,肯定其成绩,但内容应真实可信,切忌夸大其实。推荐信不要写过多空洞的内容,无须在形式上过多标新立异,但内容必须因人而异,写出特色。

1.10.2 写作步骤(Writing Steps)

1) 说明写信的目的。
2) 说明具体事由(包括被推荐人的优点及性格特点,以及写信人与被推荐人之间的关系)。
3) 表示谢意,再次表示推荐。

1.10.3 常用词汇(Vocabulary)

Shanghai Shipyard	上海船厂
scholarship	n. 奖学金
university	n. 大学
outgoing	a. 外向的
cooperative	a. 合作的
flexible	a. 灵活的
be qualified for	有资格
application	n. 申请

1.10.4 套用语句(Useful Expressions)

说明写信目的

1) I'm writing to report/recommend/introduce...
   我写信是要报告 / 推荐 / 介绍……
2) I am pleased to introduce/recommend Mr. Wang You, our manager of Textile Department.
   很高兴向您介绍 / 推荐我们纺织部的经理王有先生。

3) Allow me to introduce/recommend to you the bearer, Miss Yang Fei, daughter of an intimate friend of mine, who is going to your city to study toward the end of this month.

请允许我向您介绍／推荐持信人，杨菲小姐。她是我好友的女儿。她将去您所在的城市学习，直到这个月底。

介绍具体事由

1)说明被推荐人的优点及性格特点。

① I found that he was very…

② I have noticed that she is quite…

描述个性优点的词汇

optimistic 乐观的	curious 有好奇心的
humorous 幽默的	independent 有独立性的
warm－hearted 热心的	kind, nice 友善的
honest 诚实的	lovely 可爱的
upright 耿直的	cute 伶俐的
responsible 有责任感的	frank 坦率的
popular 有人缘的	caring 理解人的
attractive 有吸引力的	skillful and patient 循循善诱的
unselfish 无私的	gentle and understanding 温柔体贴的
modest 谦逊的	
tolerant 容忍的	industrious 勤劳的
gentle 文雅的	having a sense of responsibility 有责任感的
courageous 有勇气的	
industrious 辛勤的	learned 博学的
painstaking 刻苦的	full of humor 风趣的
generous 慷慨的	experienced 有经验的
dedicated 忠诚老实的	versatile, gifted 多才多艺的
thrifty 节俭的	caring 善解人意的
smart 聪明的	having high prestige and universal respect 德高望重的
hardworking 好学的	

2)说明写信人与被推荐人之间的关系。

① I have known…for more than…years. He was enrolled in…for…years.

我认识……已超过……年。他在……领域已有……年。

② As her…, I'm very pleased to have the opportunity to assess justly her work and personality.

作为她的……，我很荣幸有机会对她的学习和个性做出准确评价。

表示谢意,再次表示推荐,并期盼回复

1) I strongly recommend him to you, without any reservation, and appreciate your favorable consideration of his application.

我毫无保留地、强烈地向您推荐他,如蒙考虑,不胜感激。

2) I have no hesitation in recommending her and hope that you will consider her application favorably.

我毫不犹豫地将她推荐给您,希望您能考虑接受她的申请。

3) You will be appreciated if you can give her an opportunity. We are looking forward to your reply.

如果您能给她一个机会,我们将不胜感激。盼回复。

1.10.5 写作范例(Samples)

Sample 1

Dear Mr. Liu,

It is with great pleasure that I am writing this letter to recommend to you Liu Yi, a student in my department, for acceptance to your Shanghai Shipyard.

I have known Liu Yi for nearly three years. He is studying in my department and is graduating soon. He is one of the best students in my department. He is outstanding in learning. For this reason he was offered a scholarship by our university. In addition, he has a strong ability to organize social activities. For example, he was in charge of football matches and debates in our department, which were popular among students.

He is outgoing, helpful, cooperative, flexible and open-minded.

I believe he is qualified for the job and will do it better. I strongly recommend him and appreciate your favorable consideration of his application.

Sincerely Yours,
(Signature)
Zhang Wen
Professor and Dean
Department of Shipbuilding Technology
WIST

译文
例 1

> 亲爱的刘先生，
> 　　我非常高兴写信向您推荐我们系的学生刘毅去贵公司上海船厂工作。
> 　　我认识刘毅已近三年。他在我们系学习，即将毕业。他是我们系最优秀的学生之一。他学习成绩优异，经常被学院授予奖学金。除此以外，他还有很强的社会组织能力，比如他曾经负责举办过系足球赛、辩论赛，这些赛事在我系学生中非常受欢迎。
> 　　他性格外向，乐于助人，善于沟通，处事灵活而开通。
> 　　我相信他能胜任这份工作，并且会越干越好。我再次强烈向您推荐他，如蒙考虑，不胜感激。
>
> 　　　　　　　　　　　　　　　　　　　您真诚的，
> 　　　　　　　　　　　　　　　　　　　（签名）
> 　　　　　　　　　　　　　　　　　　　张文
> 　　　　　　　　　　　　　　　　　船舶技术系教授、系主任
> 　　　　　　　　　　　　　　　　　　　武汉船院

Sample 2

> Dear John,
> 　　May I recommend Mr. Robert Burks to you, who has for several years been working in English translation for more than 15 years? As his boss, I'm very pleased to have the opportunity to assess justly his work and personality. I can say frankly that he is really experienced in this field. In addition, he is an responsible and popular guy.
> 　　I strongly recommend him to you again, without any reservation, and appreciate your favorable consideration of his application.
>
> 　　　　　　　　　　　　　　　　　　　Truly yours,
> 　　　　　　　　　　　　　　　　　　　Li Ming

译文
例 2

> 亲爱的约翰，
> 　　我谨向您推荐罗伯特·伯克先生，他已从事英语翻译工作超过15年。作为他的老板，我非常荣幸有这个机会公正地评价他的工作和性格。坦率地说，他在英语翻译这个领域

真的很有经验。除此以外,他责任心强,人缘好。

我毫无保留地、强烈地向您推荐他,如蒙考虑,不胜感激。

您真诚的,

李明

1.10.6 练习(Exercises)

I. Directions: Finish the letter by choosing the proper sentences given.

A. With his outstanding leadership and cheerful personality, he was elected chairperson of the Student Union of Tsinghua University several times.

B. I am writing to recommend one of my best friends, Zhou Botong, for this post.

C. Therefore, I do not hesitate to recommend him as an ideal candidate for the post you advertised.

D. I am sure you will make a wise decision in hiring him.

E. Upon graduation he was assigned to be a teacher in Tsinghua Middle School.

F. Busy as he was, he completed his major, teenage psychology, with an outstanding school record.

G. What is more, he loves his job and enjoys working with children. This won him great popularity among his students.

Dear Sir or Madam,

Yours sincerely,

Li Ming

II. Directions: Fill in the blanks to complete the following letter of recommendation according to the Chinese given.

July 21, 2021

Dear Sir,

  _____ （我很高兴推荐李丹小姐到贵公司工作）.

  _____ （我和李小姐认识三年了）. Throughout that time, she has shown herself to be a _____ （工作努力的、有才华的）staff member of our company. Miss Li has received professional training in Australia and the U.S.A., and her expertise in her own field is unquestionable. She is an imaginative and at the same time very practical person. _____ （李小姐和蔼可亲, 和同事相处十分和睦）. She is a well-liked and valuable staff member of our company, and my colleagues all speak highly of her dedication to her work. We are in fact very sorry to lose her. _____ （我毫无保留地向您推荐她）.

                  Sincerely yours,
                  Li Ming

III. Directions: You are required to write a Letter of Recommendation according to the information given below.

  假设你是 Leah Kim。请为你的学生李明给其应聘的公司写一封推荐信，信的内容包括以下几点：

1) 介绍学生的基本情况。
2) 评价学生的表现和能力。
3) 对他未来发展的评价。

第 2 章 通知 （Notices and Announcements）

2.1 简介（Brief Introduction）

通知是广泛应用于日常生活和工作中的一种应用文体,常用于组织对所属成员布置工作或传达事务,通知分书面通知(notice)和口头通知(announcement)两种,格式各有不同。

书面通知(notice)通常张贴在学校、单位或公共场所,以书面或印刷的正式形式出现,通常用大写NOTICE以突出醒目效果。有时把发通知的单位名称和通知标题写在一起(单位名称在标题之上或包含在标题之中),这样有关人员会立刻注意到;口头通知(announcement)则以宣读或播报的方式,以声音的方式传达给听者。

2.2 书面通知（Notices）

书面通知指用文字来进行意思传达。通知一般要写上日期和发布单位,日期可写在正文的右上角,标题的下一行。如果发布单位作为通知的落款写在正文的右下角,那么日期则写在最后一行,即落款的下一行。

2.2.1 写作步骤（Writing Steps）

1) 醒目的标题,如 NOTICE,居中呈现。
2) 日期可放在标题的右下方。
3) 正文:包含通知的对象、内容、具体细节等信息。
4) 落款:写在通知的右下角,可附上时间信息。
5) 语言简洁清楚,时态多用将来时。

2.2.2 套用语句（Useful Expressions）

1)...be expected to...
　　要求……
2)...be supposed to...
　　请……

3)...be requested to...

……应该／必须……

2.2.3 写作范例(Samples)

通知发布时间为2020年10月10日,发布单位为体育馆,以下是两种不同格式的写法。告知学生从10月10日起,体育馆和所有的器材开放时间为早上9点到11点30分,下午2点30分到6点。

Sample 1

The Gymnasium
NOTICE

Oct. 10, 2020

All students are supposed to note that from Oct. 10 the Gymnasium and all the sports equipment will be available during the following hours:

9:00-11:30 a.m.
2:30-6:00 p.m.

Sample 2

NOTICE

All students are supposed to note that from Oct. 10 the Gymnasium and all the sports equipment will be available during the following hours:

9:00-11:30 a.m.
2:30-6:00 p.m.

The Gymnasium

Oct. 10, 2020

例1—2

体育馆通知

所有同学请注意:从10月10日起体育馆及全部体育器材开放时间如下:

9:00—11:30 a.m.
2:30—6:00 p.m.

2.3 口头通知(Announcements)

　　口头通知以口头传播的方式表达通知内容,比如我们日常听到的广播等。口头通知通常以一些提醒听众注意的词语或句子开始,例如:Attention, please! May I have your attention, please! 开头往往有称呼语如 Ladies and gentlemen, Comrades 等,正文部分要求以简洁明快的语言把细节交代清楚,逻辑完整。结尾处一般应加上结束语:Thank you! Thank you for listening! 以示礼貌。

2.3.1 写作步骤(Writing Steps)

1) 以称呼语开始。
2) 通知内容语言清晰流畅,逻辑完整。
3) 结束语。

2.3.2 套用语句(Useful Expressions)

1) Comrades, ...
2) Ladies and Gentlemen, ...
3) All students, ...
4) May I have your attention, please!
5) Attention, please!
6) Thank you!
7) Thank you for listening!
8) Thank you for your time!

2.3.3 写作范例(Samples)

Sample 1

　　假设你是班长,请拟定一份口头通知。要点如下:
1) 观看博物馆的展览;
2) 星期天上午8点在520路公共汽车站集合;
3) 自愿前往观看展览的同学下课后要签名。

Announcement

Boys and girls, may I have your attention, please! There is something important that you need to know. As there will be an Scientific and Technological Achievements exhibition in Wuhan Museum, we are planning to visit it this Sunday. Those who intend to go shall sign your name after class and get together at 8 a.m. on Sunday at the stop of Bus No. 520. Please don't be late. That's all. Thank you!

译文
例1

通知

同学们请注意！我有重要事情通知大家。武汉博物馆将举办科技成果展，我们计划本周日去参观。愿意去的人请课后报名，星期日上午8点在520汽车站集合，请不要迟到。谢谢大家。

Sample 2

假定你是武汉天河机场(Wuhan Tianhe International Airport)的播音员，请根据以下内容拟写一篇广播通知稿：由于早上大雾，气流不稳定，机场从安全考虑，临时决定将所有航班推迟到11点钟以后发出。各航班起飞时间已写在候机室(waiting room)的布告板(bulletin board)上。另外，因疫情影响，武汉飞往福建的所有航班已取消。凡去福建的旅客可办理退票手续。

Announcement

Ladies and Gentlemen, Attention, please!

Due to the heavy fog and unstable air flow in the morning, the airport temporarily decided to postpone all flights after 11 a.m. for safety reasons. The departure time of each flight has been written on the screen in the waiting room. In addition, due to COVID-19, all flights from Wuhan to Fujian have been cancelled. All passengers to Fujian please know.

译文
例 2

通 知
女士们、先生们,请注意: 　　由于大雾和气流影响,我们机场将推迟所有航班到上午 11 点后,今天上午的航班起飞新时间表登在候机室的电子屏幕上。因为疫情影响,到福建的所有航班已被取消,原计划飞往福建的乘客可办理退票手续。

2.4 练习(Exercises)

I. Directions: You are supposed to write an announcement according to the information given below.

假设你现在是班长,班上要举行一次英语讲座(lecture)。请用口头通知的形式把活动事项告诉同学们。

　　讲座内容:西方电影中的经典角色
　　主讲人:雅各布博士,某大学的美籍教师
　　地点:大学生活动中心
　　时间:9月25日,星期三,下午3:00—5:00

讲座后,将分组进行讨论,雅各布博士现场解惑,并回答有关英语口语学习的问题。届时请大胆提问和发言。

II. Directions: You are required to write a notice according to the information given below.
A. 假如你是学生会干部,请用英语为学生会拟一份关于开展英语活动的书面通知,内容如下。

　　a) 学生会准备组织一场英语演讲比赛(English speech contest),材料不限。
　　b) **活动目的**:提高英语口语(oral English)水平。
　　c) **活动时间**:5月5日下午2:30。
　　d) **活动地点**:大学生活动中心(activity center for college students)。

参赛者务必于4月15日前报名。欢迎全体同学参加。

B. 假定你是系部的教学秘书,请为公共课部拟一份会议通知,内容如下:

　　a) 讨论下学期教学竞赛准备事宜。
　　b) **时间**:7月15日,星期三,下午2:30。

c) **地点**:系会议室。

d) **参加人员**:公共课部全体教职工。

C. 酒店通知

尊敬的客人:

因酒店游泳池整修,明天无法提供游泳服务,其他娱乐设施可照常使用。欲知详情请致电1866。不便之处,敬请谅解!

武汉大酒店
2020年8月7日

D. 学生会(Student Union)应广大学生的要求,邀请著名跨国公司ABC Company人力资源部经理(Human Resources Manager)John Wilson先生来校为全体学生开设讲座。

内容:如何在面试中脱颖而出

时间:6月10日晚7:00—8:30

地点:图书馆活动中心

参加者:全体学生,尤其是应届毕业生

E. 假定你负责组织一个外宾团在武汉的参观游览工作,请根据以下要点拟定一份口头通知,内容如下。

a) **参观地点**:东湖、黄鹤楼、武汉大学。

b) **时间安排**:早餐后8点出发,午餐在参观地方用餐,下午5点返回。

c) 愿意去的人请在今晚10点前去服务台(Service Desk)登记。

F. Directions: The following is a NOTICE. After reading it, you're required to complete the outline below it. You should write your answers briefly (in no more than three words) in the box given below.

Notice

Over the past month the Personnel Office has received numerous calls about the approval process for using the new "flex-time" (flexible-time) working schedule. In order to know how to take advantage of this system, please keep this notice in your records.

First, you must determine if you are eligible (有资格的) to use a flex-time schedule. The flex-time system is designed for those employees those jobs do not require them to answer telephones or to be available to the public between the hours of 8:00 a.m. and 5:00 p.m. In addition, an employee must receive written permission from his or her department manager.

Then, you must submit a copy of Form FT, signed by your manager, to the Personnel Office.

The Personnel Office will notify (通知) you when approval is cleared; you may then begin your new schedule on the following Monday.

You may obtain copies of Form FT from Mary White in Room 129. If you have any questions, see your department manager—do not contact the Personnel Office directly.

Flexible Time Working Schedule

Users: employees suitable for using it

Application Process

a. Get _____ and

b. _____ a copy of Form FT to the Personnel Office, and then

c. be notified by _____.

d. Staring time: _____.

e. Contract person if there are questions: the _____.

G. Directions: You are required to write an announcement according to the following information in Chinese. You should include all the points in the following table.

事由:欢迎美国学生来我校参观

时间:6月22日上午9:00至13:00

人数:约35人

具体安排:

时间	地点	事项
8:40	校门口	集合,欢迎客人
9:00—10:00	接待室	开会欢迎,互赠礼品
10:30—11:30	校园、图书馆、实验室和语音室	参观
11:30	学生食堂	午餐
13:00	校门口	送别

第3章 海报和启事(Posters and Public Announcements)

3.1 简介(Brief Introduction)

海报和启事都是现代社会使用率较高的日常应用文书,通常以告示形式发布。一般而言,海报是一种宣传广告,内容主要是提供文体信息,例如电影放映信息、比赛讯息和演出动态等;启事是一种公告性的文体,内容主要是机关团体或个人向公众说明事情,例如寻人寻物启事、失物招领启事、更正启事、搬迁或征稿启事等。

海报和启事都要求简洁明了,短小精悍。其中,活动或者事件发生的时间、地点和人物等要素必须写清楚。有时,为了突出重点,给人以深刻印象,这些内容可以单列一行。两者的标题都位于内容的正上方,以求醒目。

3.2 海报

海报的英文标题为Poster,在正式的海报中,标题下一行往往标有活动名称;在非正式的海报中,标题即为活动名称。为了吸引公众注意,鼓励公众参与活动,海报标题的正下方一行还可以增加鼓动性的语句,例如:All are warmly welcome. The match will be wonderful!

3.2.1 写作步骤(Writing Steps)

1) 标题:Poster(海报)。
2) 活动名称。
3) 内容:活动的具体内容、时间和地点等信息。
4) 鼓动性语句。
5) 结尾:承办人或单位名称,时间有时可省略。

3.2.2 套用语句(Useful Expressions)

1) Please come and cheer for...
   欢迎前往为……助兴。
2) Catch the chance, or you will regret!

机不可失,时不再来。

3)...only if weather permits...

遇雨改期或取消。

4)...under the auspices of...

由……主办 / 由……赞助。

5) Make reservations ASAP to avoid disappointment!

预定从速,勿失良机!

6) All are warmly welcome.

欢迎大家踊跃参加。

3.2.3 写作范例(Samples)

Sample 1 (formal)

2021年5月20日星期六晚上7:30,学生会(Student Union)组织在图书馆多媒体室(multimedia room)放映科幻电影《星际穿越》(*Interstellar*),票价为十元一张。海报张贴时间为2021年5月13日。

Film News

Get your ticket now!

Splendid science fiction movie

Interstellar

Will be shown at the multimedia room of the library

At 7:30 p.m., Saturday, May 20.

With admission of 10 Yuan each.

The Student Union
May 13, 2021

译文

影讯

科幻大片《星际穿越》

5月20日周六晚7:30在图书馆多媒体室放映

入场券每张10元

欲购从速

学生会
2021.5.13

Sample 2 (informal)

电影俱乐部将于9月20日星期五晚7点整,在操场放映电影《敦刻尔克》(*Dunkirk*),入场券八元一张,售票处在俱乐部。如遇雨天,则改在体育馆放映。

FILM

Dunkirk

Time: 7:00 p.m., Fri., Sep. 20

Place: the playground

Fare: eight yuan each

Ticket officer: the film club

In case of rain, it is to be shown in the gym.

The Film Club

译文

电影

《敦刻尔克》

时间:9月20日星期五晚7:00

地点:操场

票价:8元/张

售票点:电影俱乐部

如果下雨,则在体育场放映。

电影俱乐部

3.3 启事(Public Announcements)

启事是单位或个人张贴在公共场所醒目位置,或刊登在报纸、杂志上的公开声明,要求简明扼要,准确具体。通常分为个人启事和单位启事,用于向大众或相关人士通告消息。与海报不同,启事多以连续书写的文字形式表达,符合公众惯常的阅读习惯。

3.3.1 写作步骤(Writing Steps)

1) 标题:如 LOST(寻物)、FOUND(失物招领)、MOVAL(搬迁)等;
2) 正文:主要事由、人名或者物名、时间、地点、联系方式;

3) 结尾:出启事者的姓名、公示时间等。

3.3.2 套用语句(Useful Expressions)

个人或单位启事常用语

1) The owner is expected to come to...to claim it.
   失主请到……认领。
2) The owner should get in contact with...
   失主请与……联系。
3) Those who know...are requested to report to...
   ……知情者请报告……
4) The gentlemen/lady who bought...please contact...to claim/to be refunded.
   购买了……的先生/女士,请与……联系以认领……/退款。
5) On and after May 1, the address of...will be changed to...
   自5月1日起,……的地址将变更为……
6) Please take note that we have recently moved to...
   请注意,我们最近已搬到……
7) Our address will be...
   我们的地址将是……
8) We inform you that we shall in...move to...
   我们将于……搬到……,特此通知。
9) Effective from May 16, 2021.
   自2021年5月16日生效。
10) Effective immediately, the following price changes are applicable.
    下列价格变更即时生效。
11) Effective from Oct. 1, 2020, the following products are discontinued.
    下列产品自2020年10月1日起停产。
12) Whoever has found or knows...is requested to phone...
    无论谁发现或知道……请打电话到……

3.3.3 写作范例(Samples)

3.3.3.1 个人启事(Public announcement by individuals)

A. 遗失启事

Sample 1 (formal)

五月二日早上,李书豪在7号楼504教室丢失了一件灰色外套。李书豪是二年级四班的学生。手机号:13812341234。

> LOST
> A grey overcoat was lost in Room 504 in No. 7 Building, on the morning of May 2. Please return it to the owner, Li Shuhao, Class 4, Grade 2. Tel: 13812341234.

译文

> 遗失启事
> 二年级4班的李书豪不慎将一件灰色的外套遗失在7号楼504教室。如有人拾到请拨打13812341234。

Sample 2 (informal)

遗失安踏牌白色运动挎包一只,约20厘米长16厘米宽,于四月三日星期二在图书馆丢失。如有人拾到,请拨打13443214321与失主联系。

> Lost
> A white Anta chest bag, 20cm long by 16cm wide.
> Last seen in the library, on April 3, Tuesday.
> If found, please kindly call 13843214321.

译文

> 遗失启事
> 安踏牌白色挎包,约20厘米长,16厘米宽。
> 4月3日星期二在图书馆丢失。
> 如有人拾到,请拨打13843214321与失主联系。

B. 证件丢失启事(声明)

Sample 1

王子萱是武汉大学的学生,不慎丢失了学生证,现发布证件丢失启事,声明该证件作废。

> LOST
> Wang Zixuan, from Wuhan University, lost her student identity card, No. 20210405189, which has been invalidated.

译文

> 证件丢失启事
> 王子萱,武汉大学学生,不慎丢失学生证,号码为20210405189,现声明该证件作废。

Sample 2

张佳欣的身份证丢了,现声明丢失的身份证作废。

> Lost
> Zhang Jiaxin lost his identity card, No. 420106200210010214, which has been invalidated.

译文

> 声明
> 张佳欣不慎丢失身份证,号码为420106200210010214,现声明该证件作废。

C. 寻人启事(formal)

Sample

  陈晓,女,14岁,身高1.65米,身着蓝色校服,阳光中学的学生。2021年5月15日放学后失踪。有知其下落或能提供其去向者,请尽快与附近派出所(police station)、其家人或学校联系。谢谢!家庭电话:027-34512345;学校电话:027-45623456。

> Have you seen this girl?
>   Chen Xiao, a girl of 14, about 1.65 meters tall from Sunshine Middle School, and last seen wearing a blue school uniform, was reported missing in May 15, 2021, when she failed to return home after school. Those who know her whereabouts or have information about where she is, please kindly notify a nearby police station or her family or her school as soon as possible. Thank you.
>   Home Tel: 027-34512345
>   School Office Tel: 025-45623456

译文

> **寻人启事**
> 　　陈晓,女,14岁,身高1.65米,身着蓝色校服,阳光中学的学生。2021年5月15日放学后失踪。有知其下落或能提供其去向者,请尽快与附近派出所、其家人或学校联系。
> 　　家庭电话:027-34512345
> 　　学校电话:027-45623456

D. 招领启事
Sample 1 (formal)

10月26日,李润平在阅览室发现一把雨伞。李润平是二年级五班的学生。

> **FOUND**
> 　　I happened to find an umbrella in the Reading Room this afternoon. The owner please comes to Class 5, Grade 2 to claim it. Tel: 027-87654321.
> Li Runping

Sample 2 (informal)

在建设大道捡到一只金毛犬,戴着标有Lucky姓名牌的橘色项圈。联系电话:027-44455001。

> **Found**
> Found: a golden retriever near Jianshe Avenue
> Wearing orange collar with a name tag: Lucky
> Phone: 027-44455001

3.3.3.2 单位启事 (Public announcements by organizations)
A. 停业启事 (formal)
Sample

我校第三食堂将于1月22日星期五晚餐后关门停业,并将于寒假结束后的2月25日星期一早上7:00重新开业。祝假期愉快!

> **Closure Notice**
> 　　No. 3 dining room will be closed after dinner on Friday, January 22. It will be recommenced after the winter vacation on Monday, February 25, at 7:00 am.
> 　　Enjoy your holiday!

B. 搬迁启事

Sample

阳光学院地址将于2021年9月1日变更为和平大街309号。电话:027-12344321。

Announcement
Effective from Sept 1, 2021, the address of Sunshine College will be changed to 309, Heping Street. Tel: 027-12344321

C. 退款启事(informal)

Sample

10月4日上午从阳光国际广场购买LV牌皮包的贵宾,因计算有误,多收了您的钱,请您与经理室联系以取回多收的钱。经理办公室电话:027-43211234。

Announcement
The gentleman/lady who bought an LV leather bag from Sunshine International Plaza on the morning of Oct. 4 has been overcharged through an accounting error. Will he/she please contact the Manager's Office to be refunded? Tel: 027-43211234

3.4 练习(Exercises)

Directions: You are required to write public announcements with the information given below.

A. 寻物启事

丢失物品:蓝色华为手机一部

丢失地点:学校食堂

丢失时间:7月20日(星期五)上午

失主电话:13012345678

B. 电话号码变更启事

武汉阳光有限责任公司电话号码自2021年1月1日起变更为027-87654321。地址:武汉市洪山区学苑路1号;邮编:430070。

C. 迁址启事

为响应市政府的城市规划,我公司(阳光软件)必须迁址。敬告尊敬的客户,从2022年10月1日起,我公司将在江岸区沿江大道801号开张。欢迎惠顾新址!

D. 征稿启事

1)本报的主要对象为我公司员工;出版日期为每月1日。

2)欢迎下列各种形式和体裁的稿件:

    a. 各部门情况的报道;

    b. 对我公司生产、销售、产品推广的意见和建议;

    c. 对员工业余(spare time)生活的报道;

    d. 其他报道。

3)来稿请勿超过1000字。

4)来稿如不采用,三个月内退还作者。

5)联系人:公共关系部(Public Relations Section)杨编辑。

第4章 广告(Advertisements)

4.1 简介(Brief Introduction)

广告,顾名思义,就是广而告之,即向社会广大公众告知某件事物。广义的广告包括不以营利为目的的广告,如政府公告,政党、宗教、教育、文化、市政、社会团体等方面的启事、声明等。狭义的广告(本章所涉)指以营利为目的的广告,通常指商业广告,或称经济广告,是工商企业为推销商品或提供服务,以付费方式通过广告媒体向消费者或用户传播商品或服务信息的手段。现代广告已经成为一门艺术,它种类繁多,风格各异,特点鲜明,因而也具有其独特的文体特征:词汇上,广告英语用词简洁多变、大胆新颖,多用缩写词或外来词;句法上,广告英语区别于其他应用文体,更口语化,以简单句、疑问句、祈使句、省略句为主,目的是为了朗朗上口,易记易传;修辞上,广告英语常用谐音、押韵、对偶、拟人、双关等修辞手法。

4.2 写作步骤(Writing Steps)

1) 标题(headline)。
2) 标语口号(slogan)。
3) 宣传要点(body text)。
4) 商标及插图(logo & illustration)。

4.3 套用语句(Useful Expressions)

1) elegant in shape(外观优雅)
2) carefully-selected materials(精选用料)
3) bright in color(色彩鲜艳)
4) a great variety of models(款式多样)
5) cool in summer and warm in winter(冬暖夏凉)
6) easy to use(使用方便)
7) safe to use(使用安全)

8) durable and attractive（美观耐用）

9) having high quality and reasonable price（物美价廉）

10) having a profound history and good reputation（历史悠久,久负盛名）

11) bachelor or higher degree（本科及以上学历）

12) mechanical-related major（机械相关专业）

13) preparedness to work hard, ability to learn, ambition and good health（吃苦耐劳的精神,学习能力,进取心以及身体健康）

14) good organization, interpersonal and communication skills（良好的组织、交际、沟通能力）

15) ability to work independently, mature and resourceful（独立工作的能力,成熟,应变能力强）

16) two or more years' working experience preferred（有两年或以上工作经验者优先）

17) fluent in speaking and writing English would be preferable（能用英语进行口头、书面交流者优先）

18) proficient in operating MS Office software（熟练操作办公软件）

4.4 广告中常见的缩略词（Abbreviations in Ads）

ad(s): advertisement(s) 广告
apt: apartment 公寓
bkpg: bookkeeping 登记
bl: block 街区
bnfts: benefit 救济金,抚恤金
bth: bath 浴缸
coop: cooperation 合作
Co/co: company 公司
dept: department 部门
dsh-wahr: dish washer 洗碗机
eng: engineer 工程师
exper: experience 经验
fam: family 家庭
hrs: hours 小时
gar: garage 车库
ht: heating 供热
hse: house 房屋

kit: kitchen 厨房
loc: location 地点
M/F, M-F: Monday to Friday 周一至周五
mdtwn: midtown 市中心
pdtn: production 生产
rd: road 道路
ref(s): reference 介绍信,推荐人
sal: salary 工资
schl: school 学校
secty: secretary 秘书
st: street 街道
conv: convenient 方便的
dly: daily 每日的
equlv: equivalent 对等的
f/t: full-time 全职的
furn: furnished 配有家具的
req'd: required 要求的,必要的

dble: double 双倍的
temp: temporary 暂时的
eng: engineering 工程(学)
exp: experienced 有经验的
fit: fitted 合适的,合身的

gd: good 好的
nr: near 附近的
lg: large 大的
unfurn: unfurnished 未配家具的

4.5 写作范例(Samples)

4.5.1 商业广告标语(Commercial Ads Slogans)

1) Time is what you make of it. (Swatch)
    天长地久。(斯沃琪手表)
2) Make yourself heard. (Ericsson)
    理解就是沟通。(爱立信)
3) Engineered to move the human spirit. (Mercedes-Benz)
    人类精神的动力。(梅赛德斯-奔驰)
4) Start ahead. (Rejoice)
    成功之路,从头开始。(飘柔)
5) A diamond lasts forever. (De Beers)
    钻石恒久远,一颗永流传。(戴比尔斯)
6) Fresh up with Seven-Up. (Seven-Up)
    提神醒脑,喝七喜。(七喜)
7) Intel inside. (Intel Pentium)
    给电脑一颗奔腾的"芯"。(英特尔-奔腾)

4.5.2 招聘广告 (Job Ads)

Wanted

Objective: Marketing Manager
Location: Wuhan, Hubei
Company: Walmart Stores, Inc.
Requirements
——Bachelor degree or above
——Marketing major preferred
——At least five yeas of working experience relating to sales position

—Fluent in Mandarin and English
—Good communication and presentation skills

Responsibility

—Responsible for the local management of marketing and sales activities according to the instruction from the head office
—Developing relationship with local media and customers

Contact information

HR. Department: Stella Liu

Email: Stellaliu@walmart.com

Tel: 18076498923

* Please send your résumé in both English and Chinese with a copy of your degree certificate and ID card to the email provided.

译文

招聘

工作岗位:营销经理

工作地点:湖北武汉

公司名称:沃尔玛连锁超市集团

招聘要求

——本科及以上学历

——营销专业优先

——至少五年销售相关的工作经验

——流利使用中英文

——良好的沟通和表达能力

工作职责

——根据总部指示,负责组织当地的营销和销售活动

——跟当地媒体和客户保持沟通

联系方式

人力资源部:刘女士

电子邮箱:Stellaliu@walmart.com

电话:18076498923

* 请把中英文简历、学历证书和身份证复印件发到上面的电子邮箱。

4.5.3 租赁广告(Rent Ads)

> Room for Rent
>
> An apartment with double bedrooms and one living room, near the city center, fully furnished with good environment, equipped with convenient transportation, only 5-minute walk to the subway station.
>
> Only 2000 RMB per month!
>
> Please contact Mr. Li if you are interested.
>
> Tel: 027-87865453
>
> Add: No. 111 Wuhan Jiefang Road 430040

译文

招租信息

两室一厅公寓,家具齐全,环境优雅,交通方便,毗邻市中心,到地铁站仅需步行5分钟
只需2000元/月!
如感兴趣请联系李先生。
电话:027-87865453
地址:武汉市解放大道111号 430040

4.6 练习(Exercises)

I. Directions: Decide whether the following statements are true (T) or false (F) according to the job ad.

Job Offer

Company: KFC

Position: Sales assistant-part-time

Department: Sales

Location: Nanjing

About the Position

This is a part-time position (22 hours per week). Work time is Monday afternoon, Saturday and Sunday.

Main Responsibilities

— Assisting in making sales and marketing plans every month

— Managing sales document and customer contracts using appropriate software and tools

— Receiving telephone calls and complaints

Key Requirements

— High School Diploma required, B.A. preferred

— Minimum of 2 years of sales experience

— Excellent speaking and communication skills in both Chinese and English

— Strong organizational skills

— Teamwork skills

( ) ① The job opening is offered by the Administrative Department of KFC in Nanjing.

( ) ② The sales assistant works five days a week.

( ) ③ The sales assistant need to respond to complaints from their customers.

( ) ④ Candidates with a B.A. are preferred.

( ) ⑤ No working experience is also accepted by this position.

II. Directions: You are required to translate the following ad into English.

我司现招聘兼职英语家教老师。要求英语过大学六级,有耐心,沟通能力好,有家教经验。联系人:肖老师;联系电话:027-86855432。

III. Directions: For this part, you are allowed 30 minutes to write an advertisement on your campus website to sell some of the course books/computers/bicycles you used at college. Your advertisement may include a brief description of their contents, their condition and prices, and your contact information. You should write at least 120 words but no more than 180 words.

第5章 电子邮件（Emails）

5.1 简介（Brief Introduction）

电子邮件指用电子手段提供信息交换的通信方式,是互联网应用极其广泛的服务。电子邮件综合了电话通信、邮政信件、传真等特点,通过互联网电子邮件系统,用户可以极其低廉的价格、非常快速的方式与世界上任何一个地方的互联网用户联系。

电子邮件主要由收信人地址(to)、发信人地址(from)、抄送(cc)、信件主题(subject)及附件(attachment)等构成,其中收信人的电子邮件地址是必要项目。电子邮件的"主题"应具体而简洁,因为电子邮件系统只能显示主题的三到四个词。其他各项可根据使用者的需要填写。电子邮件正文和结尾部分的格式与普通书信或便条相同。

5.2 写作模式（Writing Model）

To（收件人）
From（发件人）
Subject（主题）
Date（日期）
Body（正文）

5.3 基本特点（Basic Features）

1) 使用缩写形式,如 I'm（I am）,I'd（I would, I had）,I'll（I will）。缩写是非正式邮件的主要语言特征之一。
2) 使用直接而非间接疑问句,以求直截了当。
3) 多用动词,少用动词性名词;多用"主语+谓语+宾语"的主动式结构,少用被动式结构;多用短句,少用长句。

4）电子邮件的语言通常比较随意，但要避免使用歧视性语言（discriminatory language），尤其应注意避免"性别歧视语"。

5.4 套用语句（Useful Expressions）

4ever（forever）永远
TTYL（talk to you later）以后再聊
IYSS（if you say so）如果你这样说的话
LTNS（long time no see）好久不见
AFAIK（as far as I know）据我所知
IOW（in other words）换言之
AKA（also known as）又称

NLT（no later than）不迟于
BTW（by the way）顺便说一下
NRN（no response necessary）不必回复
FYI（for your information）供参考
WB（welcome back）欢迎归来
IMHO（in my humble opinion）依愚见
Cc（carbon copy）抄送

5.5 写作范例（Samples）

Sample 1

To： mikedd2k@163.com
From： no-eccreply@heart.org
Subject： Your Training Center Coordinator Has Confirmed Your AHA BLS Instructor Status
Date： 2016.6.2
Dear Gao Ming,   　　Congratulations! Your American Heart Association Training Center Coordinator has confirmed that you are aligned with Laerdal China Limited as a BLS Instructor. You now will be able to access content on the AHA Instructor Network by logging into the site with your username and password. This is the same username and password you entered during registration. If you have forgotten your username or password, please use the "Forgot your username or password?" link on the login page of the AHA Instructor Network. Content now available to you includes: Your personal "dashboard", including important messages and alerts from AHA Course information, updates and resources Training memos and bulletins

News, including science and Guidelines news
And much more...

Thank you for all you do to provide lifesaving training!

Sincerely,
AHA Instructor Network

译文
例1

收件人：	mikedd2k@163.com
发件人：	no-eccreply@heart.org
主题：	培训中心协调员已确认您的美国心脏协会基础生命支持导师状态
日期：	2016.6.2

亲爱的高明：

  祝贺您！美国心脏协会培训中心协调员已确认您与挪度中国有限公司合作，担任基础生命支持导师。您现在可以使用您在注册期间输入的用户名和密码登录，并访问美国心脏协会导师网上的内容。如果您忘记了用户名或密码，请使用美国心脏协会导师网登录页面上的"忘记用户名或密码"链接。您现在可以使用的内容包括：

个人"面板"，包括来自美国心脏协会的重要消息和警报
课程信息、更新和资源
培训备忘录和简报
新闻，包括科学和指南新闻
以及更多……

感谢您为提供拯救生命培训所做的一切！

您真诚的朋友
美国心脏协会导师网

Sample 2

From：	lxlex531@yahoo.bz
Date：	2021-3-28

To:huang@hotmail.com
Subject:Looking for Employees Working Remotely
Dear Mr. Huang, 　　We are looking for employees working remotely. 　　My name is Carrie. I am the personnel manager of a large international company. 　　Most of the work you can do from home, that is, at a distance. 　　The salary is $5400-$8500. 　　If you are interested in this offer, please visit our site 　　Have a nice day!

译文
例 2

发件人:lxlex531@yahoo.bz
日期:2021-3-28
收件人:huang@hotmail.com
主题:寻找线上工作员工
亲爱的黄先生, 　　我们正在寻找线上工作的员工。 　　我叫卡丽,是一家大型国际公司的人事经理。 　　大部分工作你可以在家里做,也就是说,在线做。 　　工资是5400—8500美元。 　　如果您对此报价感兴趣,请访问我们的网站。 　　祝您愉快!

5.6 练习(Exercises)

I. Directions: Fill in the blanks to complete the email according to the Chinese given.

To:Margret@sohu.com
From:Jim@sina.com
Subject:Congratulations

> **Date**: March 19, 2019
>
> Dear Margaret,
>
>   I read in the morning paper that after five years work in a Sino-American joint venture, _____(你即将开办自己的公司).
>
> Most impressive!
>
>   I would like to add my congratulations to the many you must be receiving. _____
> _____(我相信你的事业会取得巨大成功). I sincerely hope you will find in this new venture the happiness and satisfaction you so richly deserve.
>
>   Jim

II. 假定你是 Hongxia Trading Company 的雇员王东,请于 2021 年 10 月 1 日给客户 Mr. White 发一封电子邮件。

内容如下:

1) 欢迎他来武汉。

2) 告诉他已在武汉光谷金盾大酒店为他预订了房间。

3) 告诉他从天河国际机场到达武汉光谷金盾大酒店大约 42 千米左右,可以乘坐出租车或机场大巴。

4) 建议他第二天来你办公室洽谈业务。

5) 如需帮助,请电话联系。

Words for reference:

    机场大巴 shuttle bus

    天河国际机场 Tianhe International Airport

    武汉光谷金盾大酒店 Optics Valley Kingdom Plaza

III. 假定你是李明,请根据以下内容发一封电子邮件。

1) 发件人:李明。

2) 收件人:Amanda。

3) 发件人电子邮箱地址:liming@163.com。

4) 收件人电子邮箱地址:amanda@hotmail.com。

5) 发信日期:2021-10-21。

6) 事由:李明是某网上书店销售员,最近美国的 Amanda 在该书店买了一本书,书名为 *Secret to Success*。

7) 邮件涉及的内容:

① 首先感谢对方购买该书;

② 告诉客户,书已经按时寄出,预计在一周内到达;
③ 希望客户收到书后到网站上进行评价;
④ 最后推荐一些新书,欢迎该客户再次在本店选购。
  (注意:不要逐字翻译上面给出的内容提示)

第6章 备忘录和电话记录(Memos and Telephone Messages)

6.1 备忘录(Memos)

6.1.1 简介(Brief Introduction)

备忘录指任何一种能够帮助记忆,简单说明主题与相关事件的图片、文字或语音资料。它源自拉丁语 memorandum est.,意为"这是应该被记住的"。备忘录一般行文清晰,语言简介,语气坚定。

按使用对象,备忘录可分为个人备忘录、公司备忘录和外交备忘录。
1) 个人备忘录:帮助或唤起记忆的记录。
2) 公司备忘录:是书面合同的形式之一,指在买卖双方磋商过程中达成的一定程度的理解、谅解、一致意见,但不具有法律约束力。
3) 外交备忘录:其内容一般是对某一具体问题的详细说明和据此提出的论点或辩驳,以便于对方记忆或查对。另外,外交会谈中,一方为了使自己所做的口头陈述明确而不至于引起误解,在会谈末了会当面交给另一方书面纪要,这也是一种备忘录。备忘录可以在双方会谈时当面递交,也可以作为独立的文件送给有关国家,还可以附在照会、公报、声明等文件后面,作为补充文件。

随着时代的发展,备忘录的载体也不断发生变化。现在除了纸质版备忘录(便签、日记本/记事本、日历等),还有电子版备忘录(手机APP、电脑桌面端备忘录、WEB版备忘录、手机软件与WEB版相结合的云端同步备忘录等)。

6.1.2 写作步骤(Writing Steps)

1) 开头:发文日期、发文单位、收文单位、主题。
2) 正文:说明事件的具体内容。
3) 署名:一般直接签名。

6.1.3 常用词汇(Vocabulary)

```
staff      n.(全体)职员
member     n.成员
company    n.公司
department n.部门
meeting    n.会议
conference n.会议
competition n.比赛
hold       v.举行
attend     v.参加
gather     v.集合
sincerely  adv.真诚地
faithfully adv.忠实地,如实地
loyally    adv.忠诚地
```

6.1.4 套用语句(Useful Expressions)

开篇部分

1) I have the honor to inform you that...
   我很荣幸地通知您……

2) I would like to remind you that our office needs...
   我想提醒您一下,我们办公室需要……

3) I have several proposals for...
   关于……我有几个建议。

4) In response to your request for..., I have to inform you that we cannot approve the purchase.
   对于你关于……的请求,我不得不告诉你,我们不能批准。

5) This is written in response to your memo dated Nov. 11, 2009, in which you proposed that...
   回复你2009年11月11日关于……的建议。

中间部分

1) The board of directors refused your proposal/suggestion/advice at the meeting three days ago for the following reasons...
   董事会在三天前的会议上未批准你的建议,原因如下……

2) I believe these changes will...in the following ways...

我相信这些变革会通过以下方式……

结尾部分

1) 表示保持联系的常用句型。

   Please let me know your response to these suggestions.

   Please feel free to contact me if you need further information.

   If you need more information, do not hesitate to get in touch with me at any time.

   If there's any problem about this arrangement, please let me know.

2) 表示感谢的常用句型。

   I highly appreciate your consideration of these proposals.

   Your consideration of this suggestion would be appreciated.

   Further suggestions will be appreciated so that the program can be more fruitful.

6.1.5 写作格式(Writing Format)

```
           SALES DEPARTMENT
                MEMO
DATE: _____
TO: _____
FROM: _____
SUBJECT (Re): _____
     _____
     _____
     _____
     _____
     _____
     _____
                            SIGNATURE
```

6.1.6 写作范例(Samples)

Sample 1

Memo
To: All staff
From: Norman Kennedy, General Manager Office
Date: May 20, 2021
Subject: Construction of Recreation Center
The board of directors has approved the idea for a new recreation center at its meeting

this morning. We are very happy to provide facilities that will contribute to the physical fitness of all our employees.

The construction of the recreation center will begin tomorrow and shall be completed within 50 days. Each department will appoint an employee representative to collect your suggestions about activities and equipment for the recreation center.

Signature

译文
例 1

备忘录

至：全体员工
自：总经理办公室 Norman Kennedy
日期：2021年5月20日
主题：修建娱乐中心

　　今早会议上，董事会已经同意再建娱乐中心，并表示非常乐意给员工提供健身器材，让员工锻炼身体。

　　娱乐中心将于明天动工，50天内完工。每个部门都会派一个代表向员工收集关于活动和设备的建议。

签名

Sample 2

Memorandum

To: Bob Xu
From: Kevin Yao
Date: Oct. 6th, 2021
Subject: Personnel Transfer

Here are the two people transferring from our headquarters to your branch company on Oct. 6th:

a. Caroline White from the Sales Department. She is in her fourth year with SET Branch Company;

b. Donald Bush from the R & D Department. He is in his second year with our headquarters.

They will be arriving on Nov 10th. Please make arrangement for these two newcomers to have their own office. Let me know if you need more details.

Signature

译文
例2

备忘录

自：Bob Xu
至：Kevin Yao
日期：2021年10月6日
主题：人事调动
　　现在有两名同事于10月6日从总部调来分公司：
　　a. 一名同事叫Caroline White，在SET分公司的销售部门任职四年；
　　b. 另外一名同事叫Donald Bush，来自研发部门，在本公司总部任职两年。
　　请协助安排办公室。如有需要，请与总公司联系。
　　　　　　　　　　　　　　　　　　　　　　　　　　　签名

6.1.7 练习（Exercises）

I. Directions: Finish the memo by choosing the proper words or sentences given.

A. Wu Ying, Manager of Xinguang Company

B. Date

C. To

D. He asked General Manager to call him this afternoon.

E. New Food Factory

Memo

(1)：Sept. 27
(2)：General Manager
From：(3)
Subject：(4)
　　Mr. Wang Ming came here to visit general manager at 10 a.m. He hoped to talk with General Manager over the matter concerning opening a food factory in our city. Mr. Wang is to leave next Monday. (5)
　　　　　　　　　　　　　　　　　　　　　　　　　　　Signature

II. Directions: Fill in the blanks to complete the following memo according to the given Chinese.

```
                              MEMO
TO: _____(所有部门经理)
DATE: _____(2018年3月14日)
FROM: Manager of Human _____(资源)
SUBJECT: _____(年度) STAFF RETURNS
   All Department Managers _____(提醒) that the Annual Staff Returns are
required to be at the Personnel Office by 30 January. _____.
(如有困难请告之。)
                                                          Signature
```

III. Directions: Write a memo to the situation below.

假如你是一家国际大公司人力资源部的经理 Kelly Smith,你刚刚任命 Bill Thomas 为公司总部的销售经理。请给全体员工写一个备忘录,告诉他们以下内容:

宣布对 Bill Thomas 的任命;说明他开始工作的具体时间;要求总部员工准备欢迎他。

6.2 电话记录(Telephone Messages)

6.2.1 简介(Brief Introduction)

书写电话记录是办公室工作人员必须具备的一项能力。当对方要找的人不在时,你需要为对方找的人留言。电话记录要简明扼要,但又不能丢失信息,以保证信息传达的完全性。

电话记录最根本的特点是开门见山,言简意赅,切忌过长。写电话记录时,首先要对电话内容加以分析,并注意电话记录的格式和特点,把主要内容写出来即可。

6.2.2 写作步骤(Writing Steps)

1) 写清楚日期、具体时间。
2) 写清楚打电话人的姓名、身份、来电号码等。
3) 写清楚电话内容,以及是否需要回电等信息,以及如需回电的电话号码、回电时间等。

6.2.3 写作格式(Writing Format)

电话记录包括五部分:发话者(From)、收话者(To)、日期(Date)、时间(Time)、留言内容(Message)。

(注:有时还包括记录人签名)

电话记录没有具体的格式规定,公司可以根据需要设置如下简单明了的模式,以便记录。

```
                    Telephone  Message
Date: _____   Time: _____   A. M. (  )
                                              P. M. (  )
From: _____   Tel No: _____
To : _____
Message: _____
_____
_____
P.S. _____
Signed: _____
```

6.2.4 套用语句(Useful Expressions)

1)...called/rang to tell you that...
　　……打电话告诉你……
2)...said to let you know...
　　……说要让你知道……
3) ...informed you that...
　　……通知你……
4) Please call back to confirm.
　　请回电确认。
5) Call...to check if necessary.
　　如果必要,请打电话给……确认。
6) Phone and confirm when you come back.
　　回来后请打电话确认一下。

6.2.5 写作范例(Samples)

Sample 1

TELEPHONE MESSAGE
To: Danny Richard

Name of caller: Brett White
Date: 7th April   **Time:** 10:15 a.m.
Message: Meeting place with Adriana changed from Grappa's to Café Bar. Be there at 9.00 p.m.
Action: Call back if problem 01699 720 7743
Signed: Frank Churchill

译文
例1

电话记录
至:Danny Richard
自:Brett White
日期:4月7日   来电时间:早上10:15
信息内容:与Adriana的会议地点由Grappa's改到Café Bar,时间为晚上9:00。
预处理事件:如有问题请回电话,电话号码01699 720 7743。
记录人签名:Frank Churchill

Sample 2

TELEPHONE MESSAGE
To: Carla Davis
Name of caller: Mike Park
Time: 3:47 p.m.
Message: Mr. Cortes has a customer arriving on Tue. At 2:30. Flight BA502
Action: Meet the guest at the airport
Signed:
Date:

译文
例2

电话记录
至:Carla Davis
自:Mike Park

来电时间：下午 3:47
信息内容：Cortes 先生的一位客户将在周二的 2:30 到达。其乘坐飞机航班号为 Flight BA502。
预处理事件：去机场准时接客户。
记录人签名：
日期：

Sample 3

TELEPHONE MESSAGE	
From: Linda	**To**: David
Date: July, 14th	**Time**: 8:00 a.m.
Message: Linda wants you to see her off at Capital Airport this evening. So when you come back, give her a call earlier this afternoon. Her telephone number is 1367...4352.	

译文
例 3

电话记录	
自：Linda	至：David
日期：7月14日	来电时间：早上 8:00
信息内容：Linda 想要你今晚到首都机场跟她送行。因此，请你回来后，在今天下午尽早给她打个电话。她的电话号码是 1367×××4352。	

6.2.6 练习(Exercises)

I. Directions: The following is a telephone conversation and please complete the message according to the conversation.

Clare: Good afternoon. Bake Company, can I help you?
Caller: Good afternoon. Can you put me through to Karl Thomson, please?
Clare: I am afraid she is out of the office at the moment. Can I take a message?
Caller: Yes, my name is David Wolen from the Health and Safety Council.
Clare: I am sorry. Could you spell your surname, please?
Caller: W-O-L-E-N.

Clare: And it is the Health and Safety Council. Right. And what is the message, please.

Caller: I am calling about the First Aid course Ms. Thomson is arranging with us. I would like to confirm the date of beginning, May 13, but I am not...

Clare: Sorry, did you say the thirteenth or thirtieth?

Caller: The thirteenth, 13.

Clare: OK...yes...

Caller: Yes. The date is fine, but we can only take 25 participants, not 29.

Clare: So that is the First Aid Course for the week commencing 13 May and you can only take 25 people.

Caller: That's right, yes.

Clare: Right. I will give her the message.

Caller: Thanks.

Clare: You are welcome. Bye.

PHONE MESSAGE

From: _____   To: _____

Company: _____

Message: _____

_____

_____

_____

II. Directions: Please fill in the message according to the Chinese information given below.

假如你是赵明,赵钢是你的弟弟,王军是你弟弟的同学。刚才王军来电话(电话号码是86×××42)找你弟弟,恰巧他不在。请用英语写一个50词左右的电话记录,包括以下内容:

① 明天(9月9日)他们班要去八一农场帮助农民摘苹果;

② 要他穿上旧一些的衣服;

③ 告诉他早晨六点在学校门口集合,要准时,不要迟到。

From:	
To:	
Date:	
Time:	
Telephone number:	
Message:	
Signature:	

第7章 简历（Résumés）

7.1 简介（Brief Introduction）

简历是个人发送给用人单位的个人信息简介,是招聘企业了解应聘者的一张"名片",其重要性不言而喻。英文里简历称为 résumé 或 CV（curriculum vitae）. résumé 源于法语,CV 源于拉丁语,分别是 summary 和 course of life 的意思。

7.2 写作模式（Writing Model）

简历的格式较为灵活,没有统一的模板,通常根据个人的偏好和个性采用不同的样式。一般来说,简历包含如下信息:求职者姓名、性别、年龄、婚姻状况、民族、籍贯、政治面貌、联系方式、学历背景、工作经验、荣誉与成就、兴趣爱好以及自我评价等。还可以附上自己的求职信,表达自己的求职愿望以及对这份工作的理解,自身的优势与工作的匹配度等。简历不必面面俱到,以清楚简洁、条理清晰、重点突出为最佳标准。

Résumé

Name: _____   Gender: _____
Date of Birth: _____   Place of Birth: _____
Marital Status: _____   Health: _____
Address: _____
Contact Information: _____
Education background: _____
Main Courses: _____
Work Experience: _____
Personalities: _____
Interests: _____

7.3 基本特点（Basic Features）

写简历的目的是向用人单位推销自己，从而获得面试机会。因此，简历应该具有明确的目的性和针对性，条例清晰、逻辑清楚、重点突出，语气充满自信，多使用名词短语、动词短语和不完整句，通常省略句子主语。

在书写简历时，真实性至关重要。如果被发现简历中有不实或造假的信息，应聘者的形象将大打折扣，甚至直接被贴上"不诚信"的标签。其次，简历不必面面俱到，但对突出应聘者工作能力和个人成绩的部分一定要强调和凸显出来，这样才能脱颖而出，获得人力资源部门的青睐。

简历最好用 A4 标准复印纸打印，字体最好采用宋体或楷体，尽量不要用花里胡哨的艺术字体和彩色字。简历版面要简洁明快，一目了然，以一页纸为最佳。

在英文简历中，教育背景和工作经历一般采用倒叙法，即时间上由近及远，从最近的学校或工作单位开始，往前依次列举。教育背景一般包括高中及高中后教育（包括大学后继续教育），所列条目应包括学习时间、就读学校、所学专业；工作经历应列举工作时间、工作单位、个人职务／职位，也可简单列举工作内容。

7.4 套用语句（Useful Expressions）

求职目标

1) I am applying for...
   我申请……

2) Job objective：To be a...
   求职目标：成为一名……

3) Objective ：Public relations manager
   求职目标：公关经理

4) Position desired：Teacher of English
   理想职位：英语教师

5) Position applied：Lecturer/Instructor of English
   申请职位：英语教师

教育背景

1) Completed 10 courses in...
   修完10门……课程

2) Graduated from...Department,...University, receiving the degree of...in...
   毕业于……大学……系,获……学……学位
3) Completed...courses at...University
   在……大学修完……课程
4) Received certificate in...
   获……证书
5) Trained in...
   受过……培训
6) Have successfully completed...training program in...
   顺利修完……培训班的……课程
7) Have taken and passed courses in...at...University
   在……大学学习……并通过考试
8) Graduated cum laude
   以优异的成绩毕业
9) Bachelor of Arts in English Language Education at Wuhan University (July 2008)
   武汉大学英语教育文学学士(2008.7)
10) Harvard University Boston, Massachusetts, USA 1998-2009
    1998—2009 美国马萨诸塞州波士顿哈佛大学

工作经历

1) participate in...
   参加……
2) taught courses in...
   教授……课程
3) worked as a(n)...
   担任……
4) conducted research on...
   从事……的研究
5) organized English corner on campus
   组织校园英语角
6) currently teaching English Writing in...University
   现在……大学教英语写作
7) appointed director of...
   被任命为……主任
8) responsible for...
   负责……

9) sales manager at...company

   任……公司销售经理

10) associate professor at...teaching American Literature

    ……大学副教授，教授美国文学。

所获奖励

1) Excellent Student Award (2019-2020)

   优秀学生／三好学生(2019-2020)

2) First prize for the English speech contest

   英语演讲比赛一等奖

3) Recipient of a second-class scholarship

   二等奖学金获得者

4) Winner of the first prize of the 2020 Nation English Contest for College Students

   2020年全国大学生英语竞赛一等奖获得者

5) University's third-class scholarship

   校三等学金

外语水平

1) Able to converse in simple English

   能用简单的英语交流

2) Can use conversational English

   会使用日常英语会话

3) Certificate for College English Test, Band 4/6 (CET 4/6)

   大学英语四／六级考试证书

4) National Computer Rank Test, Grade 1

   全国计算机等级考试一级

5) Passed the Test for English Majors, Grade 4 in Spring 2018

   通过了2018年大学英语专业四级考试

6) Scored 680 in CET 4 in 2019

   2019年大学英语四级考试680分

7) Business English Certificate (BEC)

   剑桥商务英语证书

8) Test of English as a Foreign Language (TOEFL) 668, TWE 5.3

   托福考试668分，写作5.3分

9) International English Language Testing System (IELTS)

   雅思考试

10) English (Fluent in both speaking and writing)
    英语(口语流利,笔头能力强)

11) Limited use of Russian
    略懂俄语

12) Basic familiarity with Italian
    略懂意大利语

13) Japanese (reading only)
    日语(仅能阅读)

14) French (Basic reading and writing)
    法语(具备基本的阅读能力和写作能力)

15) English: Fairly good reading ability
    英语:有较强的阅读能力

16) Excellent/skillful/good reading/writing ability
    阅读 / 写作能力很强 / 较强

17) Can participate in discussions in English
    能用英语进行讨论

7.5 写作范例(Samples)

例1

姓　　名:张庆　　　　　　性　别:男
出生年月:1988年5月8日　　籍　贯:湖北武汉
婚姻状况:已婚　　　　　　健康状况:佳
家庭住址:湖北省武汉市汉阳区琴台大道101号
联系电话:13384758543
电子邮箱:zhangqing@sohu.com
教育背景:2003—2006　武汉市第六高级中学
　　　　　2006—2010　武汉大学英语系
工作背景:2010至今　武汉二中英语教师
个人爱好:旅行、读书

译文

Sample 1

RÉSUMÉ

Name: Zhang Qing **Gender:** male
Date of Birth: May 8th 1988 **Place of Birth:** Wuhan Hubei
Marital Status: Married **Health:** Excellent
Address: 101, Qintai Road, Hanyang District, Wuhan, Hubei
Mobile: 13384758543
Email: zhangqing@sohu.com
Education:
  2006-2010 Department of English, Wuhan University
  2003-2006 Wuhan No. 6 Senior Middle School
Work Experience:
  2010 to present English teacher of Wuhan No. 2 Middle School
Personal hobbies: travel, reading

Sample 2

RÉSUMÉ

Full Name: Qiao Shulei
Address: No. 105 Yingwu Road, Hanyang District, Wuhan, Hubei
Date of Birth: April 25, 1977
Sex: Female
Marital Status: Single
Health: Excellent
Education:
  1996-1999 Wuhan Institute of Shipbuilding Technology
    (Major: Shipbuilding and Repairing)
  1990-1996 No. 2 High School, Huanggang, Hubei

Work Experience:
  Nov. 2001 to present Engineer (Huangpu Shipbuilding Industry Co. Ltd)
  July 1999-Oct. 2001 Assistant Engineer
    (Qingdao Shipbuilding Industry Co. Ltd)

译文
例2

简历	
姓　　名	乔书蕾
地　　址	武汉市汉阳区鹦鹉大道105号
出身年月	1977.4.25
性　　别	女
婚姻状况	未婚
健康状况	健康
教育背景：	
1990—1996	湖北省黄冈二中
1996—1999	武汉船舶职业技术学院（专业：船舶制造与维修）
工作经历：	
1999.7—2001.10	助理工程师（青岛造船厂）
2001.11至今	工程师（黄浦造船厂）

7.6 练习（Exercises）

I. Directions: Fill in the following résumé according to the information given below.

胡斌，男，未婚，身体健康，1989年3月出生于辽宁省大连市，2007年7月从武汉船舶职业技术学院船舶制造与维修专业毕业。爱好唱歌、足球与旅游。

2009年3月至7月，在哈尔滨工程大学进行船舶制造与维修专业培训，获培训证书。2007年7月至2009年2月在大连造船厂任助理工程师。2009年9月至今，在大连船舶工程研究所任工程师。

其他相关资料备索。

欲寻求与船舶制造相关的工作。

地址：辽宁省大连市和平大道86号

电话：0411-66654320

Hu Bin

86 Hepin Road, Dalian, Liaoning Province, China

Tele: 0411-66654320

Job Objective

Education and Training
_____
_____
_____

Work Experience
_____
_____
_____

Personal Data
    Born: _____
    Sex: _____
    Health: _____
    Marital state: _____
    Interests: _____

References
_____

II. Directions: Translate the following into Chinese.

RÉSUMÉ

Li Xizhe
Letter Box 975
Wuhan University
Wuhan, Hubei(430005)
Tel: 027-87688789
Mobile: 13271269603
Email: lxz2009@sohu.com

OBJECTIVE
To be a college English teacher

EDUCATION
2002 to present Foreign Language College, Wuhan University
               MA in English Language and Literature (Degree expected in July this year)
1999-2002   No. 5 Middle School, Wuhan

SOCIAL EXPERIENCE

Aug. 2008	Volunteer for the Beijing Olympic Games
2003-2006	Part-time interpreter for Wuhan University's Foreign Affairs Office
2002-2004	Editor of the Campus English Newspaper

CERTIFICATES

2006	Certificate for Test for English Majors, Grade 8 (TEM 8)
	Certificate for Oral Test of TEM 4
2005	National Computer Rank Test Certificate, Grade 2

HONORS

2008	Excellent Student Award
2007	Winner of the first prize of the 2007 National Contest for College Students
2005	First prize, Government Scholarship
2004	Second prize for English Drama Contest

HOBBIES

Listening to music, traveling, painting, calligraphy

PERSONAL DATA

Sex	Male
Marital Status	Single
Date of Birth	Dec 23, 1983
Health	Good
Height	178cm
Weight	65kg

REFERENCES

Available upon request

III. Directions: Suppose you will soon graduate from university, prepare a résumé for job application.

第8章 说明书(Instructions)

8.1 简介(Brief Introduction)

说明书属于科技应用文,用来说明产品的特点、性能、用途、用法、成分、储藏方法及使用期限等。说明书为正式文体,应逻辑严密、科学性强,层次清楚。说明书语言简洁明了,一般不用修辞手法,句子结构简单,常使用祈使句、被动语态,多省略冠词、介词及无关紧要的形容词、副词、连词等,多使用科技术语,常用复合名词词组代替后置定语。本章主要介绍药品、食品和日用品说明书的书写。

8.2 套用语句(Useful Expressions for Instructions)

成分

1) consist of...
   由……组成
2) be obtained from...
   由……制得
3) contain...
   含有……
4) be prepared from...
   由……制备
5) have (possess)...
   有(具有)……

适应证

1) be active against...
   对……有效
2) be intended to...
   适用于……
3) be effective in (for, against)...
   对……有效

4) be recommended for…
    推荐用于……

5) be employed to…
    用于……

6) be indicated in (for)…
    适用于……

7) for (in) the treatment (management) of…
    用于治疗(控制)……

注意事项

1) be contraindicated in (for)…
    对……禁忌

2) should not be used (employed) in…
    不得用于……

3) It is advisable to avoid the use of…
    建议不用于……

4) must not be administered (given) to…
    对……不得用药

5) should be used with caution
    慎用

6) be not recommended for…
    最好不用于……

用药方式

take 服用　　inhale 吸入　　apply to 用于,涂于,敷于

spray 喷雾　　inject 注射　　swallow 吞服

储存

1) store (keep) in a cool and dry place
    置于阴凉干燥处

2) away from light
    避光

3) away from children/out of (the) reach of children
    勿让儿童接触

4) protect from light (heat)
    避光(热)

5) prevent moisture
    防潮

8.3 药品说明书(Drug Instructions)

8.3.1 写作模式(Writing Model)

药品名称(Drug Name)

成分(Ingredients/Contains):
性状(Feature/Description/Composition/Introduction):
药理作用(Pharmacological Action):
适应证(Indications):
疗效(Functions):
用法用量(Directions/Application/Dosage and Administration):
禁忌证(Contraindications):
不适应人群(People Not Intended for):
注意事项(Warnings/Precautions/Cautions/Notes):
不良反应(Side Effects/Adverse Reaction/Side Reaction/By-Effects):
有效期(Validity Term/Shelf Life/Expiration Date):
储存(Storage):
包装(Package):

8.3.2 写作范例(Samples)

Sample 1

Itch-Relieve Ointment

Ingredients: Borneol, mint
Functions: Relieve skin irritation; improve skin metabolism
Application: Apply to the affected part; several times a day
Warnings: Never apply it to face; wait a few days between each tube
Validity Term: One year
Storage: Keep out of children's reach; avoid strong light

译文
例 1

止痒膏
成分：冰片、薄荷
疗效：治疗皮肤瘙痒,改善皮肤新陈代谢
用法：涂抹患处,一日数次
注意事项：切勿用于面部,每用完一管后间隔几日
有效期：一年
储存：勿让儿童接触,避开强光

Sample 2

Nurofen Recovery
Functions: Delivering effective relief from headaches   **Features**:   Dissolving quickly on the tongue   **People Not Intended for**:   ① Patients with an allergic reaction to aspirin   ② Patients having asthma when taking aspirin   ③ Children under the age of 12   **Dosage**:   ① Starting Dose: 2 tablets   ② If necessary: Take 1 or 2 tablets every 4 hours   ③ Maximum daily intake: 6 tablets   **Possible Side Effects**:   ① Stomach discomfort   ② Worsening of asthma   ③ Shortness of breath

译文
例 2

纽洛芬去痛片

疗效：
　　有效缓解头痛

特性：
　　于舌头上快速溶解

不适应人群：
　　① 对阿司匹林过敏者
　　② 服用阿司匹林产生哮喘者
　　③ 12 岁以下儿童

剂量：
　　① 首次量：2 片
　　② 如有必要：每 4 小时 1—2 片
　　③ 最大日剂量：6 片

不良反应：
　　① 胃部不适
　　② 哮喘加重
　　③ 呼吸短促

8.4 食品说明书（Food Instructions）

8.4.1 写作模式（Writing Model）

食品名称（Product Name）

配料（Ingredients）：

适用人群（Suitable Users）：

使用方法（Directions）：

储藏（Storage）：

保质期至／此日期前最佳（Best Before）／保质期（Shelf Life）：

生产日期（Manufacturing Date）：

生产商（Manufacturer）：

执行标准（Product Standard Code）：

8.4.2 写作范例(Samples)

Sample 1

KRAFT RITZ SANDWICH CRACHER

Ingredients: Wheat flour, non-hydrogenated vegetable oil, peanut butter, whey powder, sugar, high-fructose syrup, salt, acidity regulator, emulsifier, enzymes

Suitable Users: Good for both young and old

Storage: Keep in a cool and dry place; avoid direct sunlight

Best Before (Y/M/D): 2022/3/18

Manufacturing Date: 2021/3/18

Manufacturer: Nabisco Foods (Suzhou) Co. Ltd.

　　　　　　　Address: 51 Baiyu Road, Suzhou Industrial Park, Jiangsu, China

Product Standard Code: Q/NSL018

译文

例1

卡夫·乐滋芝士夹心饼干

配料: 小麦粉、非氢化植物油、花生酱、乳清粉、糖、高果糖糖浆、盐、酸度调节剂、乳化剂、酶类

适用人群: 老少皆宜

贮藏: 请置于干燥凉爽处,避免阳光直射

保质期至／此日期前最佳: 2022/3/18

生产日期: 20021/3/18

生产商: 纳贝斯克食品(苏州)有限公司

　　　　地址:中国江苏省苏州工业园区白榆路51号

执行标准: Q/NSL018

Sample 2

Lay's Italian Red Meat Flavor Potato Chips

Ingredients: Potatoes, vegetable oil, Italian red meat flavor seasoner (powdered soy, white sugar, whey powder, salt, monosodium glutamate, onion powder, spice, food flavor, anti-tacking agent, citric acid, artificial sweetener (with phenylalanine), allura red, 5′-disodium 5′-guanylate, disodium inosinate)

Storage: Keep in a cool and dry place; avoid direct sunlight. To prevent moisture, eat up instantly after opening the package

Shelf Life: 9 months

Manufacturing Date: 2021/5/20

Manufacturer: Lay's Foods (China) Co. Ltd.
　　　　　　　Address: 99 Dongxing Road, Songjiang Industrial Park, Shanghai, China
　　　　　　　Post Code: 201800

Product Standard Code: QB/T2686

译文
例2

乐事意大利香浓红烩味薯片

配料: 马铃薯、植物油、意大利香浓红烩味调味料(酱油粉、白砂糖、乳清粉、食用盐、谷氨酸钠、洋葱粉、香辛料、食用香料、抗结剂、柠檬酸、甜味素(含苯丙氨酸)、诱惑红、5′-鸟苷酸二钠、5′-肌苷酸二钠)

贮藏: 请置于干燥凉爽处,避免阳光直射;开袋后请即食,以免受潮

保质期: 9个月

生产日期: 2021/5/20

生产商: 乐事食品(中国)有限公司
　　　　　地址:上海市松江工业园东兴路99号　邮编:201800

执行标准: QB/T2686

8.5 日用品说明书(Necessity Instructions)

8.5.1 写作模式(Writing Model)

产品名称(Product Name)
简介(Brief Introduction):
使用方法(Directions):
注意事项(Cautions):
主要成分(Ingredients):
贮藏(Storage):
警告(Warnings):
执行标准(Product Standard Code):
产地(Place of Origin):
保质期至/此日期前最佳(Best Before):

8.5.2 写作范例(Samples)

Sample 1

Oral-B Sensitive Toothpaste with Fluoride

Oral-B Sensitive Toothpaste with Fluoride contains a clinically proven ingredient to reduce the pain of teeth sensitive to heat, cold, or pressure. It is formulated to be less abrasive, so it is mild and gentle to enamel, gums and exposed dentin. It contains fluoride for continued protection against cavities. And, its refreshing flavor leaves your mouth feeling clean and minty fresh.

Directions: Use twice a day or as recommended by your dentist. Brush thoroughly, especially at the gum line. Regular use will help provide continued protection against sensitivity

Cautions: Sensitive teeth may indicate a serious problem that may need prompt care by a dentist. See your dentist if the problem persist or worsens

Ingredients: potassium nitrate 5.00%, sodium fluoride 0.200%, cellulose gum, glycerin, mint, flavor, water

Storage: Store below 30℃

Warnings: Keep out of reach of children
Place of Origin: Made in the Netherlands
Best Before (Y/M/D): 2021/12/16

(——摘自晨梅梅主编《实用写作教程》p245)

译文
例1

欧乐-B抗过敏牙膏（含氟配方） 　　经临床验证，欧乐-B抗过敏牙膏能有效减少牙齿因热、冷或触压所引起的疼痛。其配方腐蚀性较小，性质温和，能减少对牙齿珐琅质、牙龈及裸露的牙本质的磨损。它的含氟配方能持续保护牙齿，防止蛀牙。此外，清凉的薄荷口味，使您的口腔清爽、口气清新。 **使用方法：**每日使用两次，或遵医嘱。刷牙要彻底，尤其是牙龈部分。经常使用能为敏感性牙齿提供持续保护 **注意事项：**牙齿过敏可能提示严重问题，需要牙医及时治疗。如果症状持续或恶化，请去牙医处就诊 **主要成分：**硝酸钾5.00%、氟化钠0.200%、纤维素羧甲醚(稳定剂)、甘油、薄荷、香料、水 **贮藏：**30℃以下保存 **警告：**请置于儿童接触不到的地方 **产地：**荷兰 **保质期至／此日期前最佳：**2021/12/16

Sample 2

AUPRES BALANCING CLEANING FOAM 　　This cleaning foam washes away impurities and old surface cells while retaining moisture to leave the skin feeling silky smooth 　　Forms a fine, rich lather that removes impurities, excess sebum and loose surface cells 　　Gently removes impurities to heighten the skin's ability to absorb moisture 　　Washes away gently to leave the skin feeling dewy-fresh, never tight **Directions:** First wet your face. Squeeze out approx. 1cm of cleansing foam into your palm and work up a rich lather with cool or lukewarm water. Gently smooth over the face suing circular motions. Rinse well **Cautions:** Rinse carefully along the hair and jaw line to remove all traces of foam. Avoid contact with eyes. If contact occurs, rinse eyes thoroughly with water

Ingredients: AMT, Xylitol, beeswax, glycerine, lycine etc.
Product Standard Code: Q/YQ047086
Place of Origin: Made in Japan
Best Before (Y/M/D): 2021/12/28

译文
例2

欧伯莱均衡洁面膏

均衡洁面膏能彻底清除陈旧的角质及肌肤污垢,同时保持肌肤滋润,使肌肤光滑洁净
产生柔和丰富的泡沫,洗净污垢和多余的皮脂、陈旧的角质
温和清除肌肤污垢,令肌肤更易吸收滋润成分
感触柔滑,用后无紧绷感,令肌肤莹润滑爽
使用方法: 现将面部淋湿,然后从软管中取1cm于掌心,加少量清水或温水揉至产生丰富泡沫,在面部轻柔地划画圈清洗,最后用清水或温水充分冲洗干净
注意事项: 特别注意发迹和下巴处,请重复冲洗干净。避免接触眼睛,如不慎进入眼内,请立即用清水冲洗干净
主要成分: ATM、木糖醇、蜂蜡、甘油、甜菜碱等
执行标准: Q/YQ047 086
产地: 日本
保质期至/此日期前最佳: 2021/12/28

8.6 练习（Exercises）

I. Directions: Fill in the blanks to complete the following instructions according to the Chinese given.

Cinnamon Leaf Oil

Ingredients: Cinnamon leaf oil and other inflammation reducers
_____(疗效)**:** For bone & muscular aches, fracture swelling, sprains

Administration: _____（仅外用）. Apply and rub over affected part frequently
Warnings: _____（避免直接接触眼睛）
_____**（有效期）:** Two years
Storage: Keep tightly sealed in cool place

II. Directions: Translate the following instructions into Chinese.

Fenbid Capsule

Indications: For the relief of severe pain and inflammation due to various causes
Administration: Take one capsule, twice daily, morning and evening
Cautions: Before giving to children under 12, consult a doctor. Overdose may cause headache and sickness
Duration: Three years
Storage: Keep in a cool and dry place

第9章 日程和计划安排表（Agendas and Programs）

9.1 简介（Brief Introduction）

　　日程和计划安排表主要用于大型会议活动、旅游行程、课程表、演出节目安排，航班、火车、汽车、轮船时刻安排等。
　　英文日程表的格式和汉语日程表相似，注重格式排列，简洁明了，通常以主要内容为标题，正文为活动内容、日程、行程，有时还包括注意事项等。
　　日程和计划安排表一般使用祈使句、省略句或不完整句子，且大量使用名词词组。

9.2 写作模式（Writing Model）

Agenda/Schedule/Timetable/ Program for_____（日程或计划安排表名称）	
Time(and place)	Event

9.3 写作范例（Samples）

9.3.1. 会议日程(Meeting Agendas)

Sample 1

Agenda for the Meeting of the Board of Directors	
Time and place: To be held in the boardroom at 9:00 a.m. on Monday, 26th October	**Content:** ① To consider the quotation received from ABC Computer Company for the supply of CPU. ② To consider the applications received from the post of assistant engineers.

	③ To consider the possibility of establishing a staff club for the junior staff of the company. ④ Any other business.

译文
例 1

董事会议日程	
时间、地点： 于10月26日星期一上午9：00董事会会议室举行	内容： ① 讨论来自ABC电脑公司有关CPU的报价。 ② 讨论公司助理工程师一职的求职申请。 ③ 讨论为公司初级职员成立俱乐部的可能性。 ④ 其他事宜。

Sample 2

Schedule for World Conference on Translation Shanghai July 2-4	
July 2 (Mon.) 8:00-11:30 11:30-13:30 13:30-14:00 14:00-15:00 15:00-15:30 15:30-17:00	Registration Lunch Plenary Session: Opening ceremony Review of Translation in China by Prof. Li Dan Intermission Mechanical Translation by Prof. Peter White
July 3 (Tue.) 8:30-10:00 10:00-10:30 10:30-11:00 11:30-13:30 13:30-17:30	Parallel Sessions: Discussion Coffee Break Plenary Session: Slides & Videos Lunch Visiting Language Translation Center

July 4 (Wed.)	8:30-10:00	Workshop Sessions
	10:00-10:30	Intermission
	10:30-11:30	Workshop Sessions
	11:30	Adjournment
	12:00	Dinner Party

译文

例2

<div align="center">**世界翻译大会日程**</div>	
	<div align="right">上海</div><div align="right">7月2日—7月4日</div>
7月2日（星期一）	
8:00—11:30	报到
11:30—13:30	午餐
13:30—14:00	全体会议：开幕式
14:00—15:00	李丹教授做有关《回顾中国翻译》的报告
15:00—15:30	休息
15:30—17:00	怀特·彼得教授做有关《机器翻译》的报告
7月3日（星期二）	
8:30—10:00	分组会议：讨论
10:00—10:30	休息
10:30—11:00	全体会议：观看幻灯片和视频
11:30—13:30	午餐
13:30—17:30	参观语言翻译中心
7月4日（星期三）	
8:30—10:00	专题讨论会
10:00—10:30	休息
10:30—11:30	专题讨论会
11:30	休会
12:00	宴会

9.3.2. 旅游行程表(Itineraries)

Sample

	Schedule for Guests to Wuhan	
May 1 (Fri.)	8:00	Meet in the hotel lobby
	8:20	Go on excursion to the Moshan Mountain Scenic Spots
	11:00	Go sightseeing along the East Lake
	12:00	Back to hotel for lunch
	14:00	Visit the famous Yellow Crane Tower
	17:00	Dinner at a restaurant in Hubuxiang Lane
May 2 (Sat.)	8:30	Tour around the Yuehu Lake Scenic Spots
	10:30	Visit Guiyuan Temple
	12:00	Have lunch at the restaurant of Guiyuan Temple
	13:00	Visit Wuhan Zoo
	16:00	Take a walk along the Hanyang Beach Park
	17:30	Dinner at Qingchuan Holiday Inn
May 3 (Sun.)	8:30	Go on excursion to the Hankou Beach Park
	10:30	Visit Zhongshan Park
	12:00	Have lunch at a restaurant in Jiqing Street
	14:30	Go shopping in the Jianghan Road pedestrian mall
	17:30	Dinner at Tianan Holiday Inn
	19:40	To the Airport

译文

例

	武汉游客日程安排表	
5月1日(星期五)		
	8:00	酒店大堂集合
	8:20	游览磨山风景区
	11:00	沿东湖观光
	12:00	回酒店吃午餐
	14:00	游览著名的黄鹤楼
	17:00	于户部巷吃晚餐

5月2日(星期六)	
8:30	游览月湖风景区
10:30	参观归元寺
12:00	于归元寺餐厅吃午餐
13:00	武汉动物园游玩
16:00	汉阳江滩公园散步
17:30	晴川假日酒店用晚餐
5月3日(星期天)	
8:30	游览汉口江滩
10:30	中山公园游玩
12:00	于吉庆街吃午餐
14:30	江汉路步行街购物
17:30	天安假日酒店用晚餐
19:40	去机场

9.3.3. 课程表(Curriculum Schedules)

Sample

Curriculum Program for the 1st Academic Year			
The First Term		The Second Term	
Courses	Credits	Courses	Credits
Philosophy of Marxism	2	College English	3
Introduction to Law	3	Mathematics	3
College English	3	Physical Education	2
Physical Education	2	Principle of Accounting	4
Mathematics	3	Accounting Information Systems	4
Introduction to Computer Science	2	Reckoning by the Abacus	3
Domestic Affairs & Policies	1	Introduction to Mao Zedong Thought	1

译文
例

第一学年课程计划表			
第一学期		第二学期	
课程名称	学分	课程名称	学分
马克思主义哲学原理	2	大学英语	3
法律基础	3	数学	3
大学英语	3	体育	2
体育	2	会计学原理	4
数学	3	会计信息系统	4
计算机导论	2	珠算	3
形势与政策教育	1	毛泽东思想	1

9.3.4. 演出节目表(Programs)

Sample

Program of National Day Entertainment Performance	
Acts	Performers
Chorus: *My Motherland*	Members from the Labor Union
Waltz: *Auld Lang Syne*	Teachers from the English Department
Folk Song: *Spring Story*	Li Li, teacher from the math teaching group
Recitation: *Nostalgia*	Liu Dong, teacher from the College of Liberal Arts
Female Solo: *Qinghai-Tibetan Plateau*	Liu Li, student from Wuhan Conservatory of Music
Cross-Talk: *Yesterday, Today and Tomorrow*	Students from Class 2111
Martial Art Performance: *Chinese*	Students from the Dynamic Engineering Department

译文
例

国庆节文艺演出节目单	
节目	表演者
合唱:《我的祖国》	工会成员
华尔兹:《友谊地久天长》	英语系教师
民歌:《春天的故事》	数学教研组教师 李力
朗诵:《乡愁》	文学院教师 刘东
女声独唱:《青藏高原》	武汉音乐学院学生 刘莉
相声:《昨天、今天、明天》	2111班学生
武术表演:《中国人》	动力工程系学生

9.3.5. 班车时刻表(Timetables)

Sample

Timetable for Wuhan Tianhe Airport Shuttle Buses				
Runtime: 6:00-22:00				
Fujiapo Bus Station	Qingnian Road Station	Hangkong Road Station	Jinjiadun Bus Station	Hankou Minhang Community Station
6:00	6:30	6:20	6:40	6:40
6:40	7:20	6:40	7:00	6:50
7:20	8:10	7:00	7:20	7:00
8:00	8:50	7:40	8:00	7:20
8:40	9:20	8:40	9:00	7:40
9:20	10:00	9:40	10:00	8:20
10:00	10:40	10:40	11:00	8:30
10:30	11:10	11:40	12:00	9:10
⋮	⋮	⋮	⋮	⋮
20:00	18:50	17:40	18:00	22:00

译文
例

武汉天河机场班车时刻表					
运行时间：6:00-22:00					
付家坡汽车站	青年路站	航空路站	金家墩汽车站	汉口民航小区站
6:00	6:30	6:20	6:40	6:40
6:40	7:20	6:40	7:00	6:50
7:20	8:10	7:00	7:20	7:00
8:00	8:50	7:40	8:00	7:20
8:40	9:20	8:40	9:00	7:40
9:20	10:00	9:40	10:00	8:20
10:00	10:40	10:40	11:00	8:30
10:30	11:10	11:40	12:00	9:10
⋮	⋮	⋮	⋮	⋮
20:00	18:50	17:40	18:00	22:00

9.4 练习（Exercises）

I. Directions: Translate the following Schedule into Chinese.

MANAGER WANG'S SCHEDULE	
November 2（Monday）	
8:30 a.m.	Make an appointment with Mr. White
4:30 p.m.	Pick up Mr. Blaire at the airport
November 3（Tuesday）	
9:30 a.m.	Show Mr. Blaire around the plant
2:30 p.m.	Discuss contracts with Mr. Blaire
November 4（Wednesday）	
9:00 a.m.	Write a performance report
4:00 p.m.	Attend the staff meeting
November 5（Thursday）	
10:00 a.m.	See exhibition in the Arts Museum

2:30 p.m.	Attend a business meeting
November 6 (Friday)	
9:00 a.m.	Pick up Mr. Blaire to the airport

II. Directions: Write a meeting agenda based on the information given in Chinese.

中美合资 LJ 电脑公司(LJC)将于 2021 年 12 月 10 日在武汉市武珞路 385 号的五月花(Mayflower)酒店召开年度全体股东大会。请根据以下内容拟定一份大会日程表。

大会在 8:30 开始,12:00 结束。
议题如下:
① 报到登记 15 分钟;
② 会议开幕式 15 分钟;
③ 欢迎和介绍 15 分钟;
④ 管理委员会(Managing Board)2020 年财政年度报告 45 分钟;
⑤ 监理会(Supervisory Board)2020 年财政年度报告 45 分钟;
⑥ 休息 15 分钟;
⑦ 利润分配 30 分钟;
⑧ 提问 30 分钟;
⑨ 会议结束。
联系电话:027-68871588。

**Annual General Meeting of Shareholders
of Sino-America LJ Computer**

To be held on _____ at _____
TEL: _____

Time	Agenda

第10章　合同和协议（Contracts and Agreements）

10.1 简介（Brief Introduction）

　　合同又叫契约,是平等主体之间设立、变更、终止民事权利义务关系的协议。协议是社会生活中协作双方或数方为保障各自的合法权益,经双方或数方共同协商达成一致意见后,签订的书面材料。

　　合同和协议是公务、商贸及其他社会活动中必不可少的正式文体形式。由于具有法律效力,合同和协议的所有条款必须表达明确,语言严谨,行文规范。在拟定合同和协议时,应保证语言与数据的准确性,避免引起误解和产生歧义。

10.2 写作步骤（Writing Steps）

1) 标题:合同/协议的名称。
2) 前言:合同/协议的编号、签约日期、地点、当事人的名称、联系方式、缔约目的、原则等。
3) 正文:双方签约的内容,包括货物的名称、品质、数量、价格、保险、当事人的权利和义务、违约赔偿、争议解决等条款。
4) 最后条款:合同/协议有效期、合同双方法人代表签字和备注等。

10.3 常用词汇（Vocabulary）

```
negotiation   n. 协商,谈判
contract      n. 合同
agreement     n. 协议,协定
valid         adj. 有效的
validity      n. 有效,合法性
expiry        n. 满期,逾期
null          adj. 无法律效力的,失效的
```

> void   *adj.* 无效的
> authorized   *adj.* 权威认可的,经授权的
> representative   *n.* 代表
> authentic   *adj.* 真正的,可靠的
> stipulate   *v.* 制订,规定
> commence   *v.* 开始
> terminate   *v.* 结束,使终结

10.4 套用语句(Useful Expressions)

1) After friendly negotiations, both sides have entered into this contract/agreement on the following terms and conditions.

  经友好协商,双方就以下条款签订该合同／协议。

2) The duties of…are as follows…

  ……的义务或职责如下……

3) The contract shall be valid for 2 years from the effective date of the contract; on the expiry of the validity term of contract, the contract shall automatically become null and void.

  本合同有效期从合同生效之日起共2年,有效期满后,本合同自动失效。

4) This contract is signed by the authorized representatives of both parties on Dec. 9, 2020.

  本合同由双方代表于2020年12月9日签订。

5) The contract is made out in English and Chinese in quadruplicate, both texts being equally authentic, and each party shall hold two copies of each text.

  本合同用英文和中文两种文字写成,一式四份。双方执英文本和中文本各一式两份,两种文字具有同等效力。

6) The representatives of Party A and Party B have agreed to conclude this contract according to the terms and conditions stipulated below:…

  甲乙双方代表同意订立本合同,条款如下:……

7) This agreement is to remain valid for…, commencing on…and terminating on….

  本协议有效期为……,从……开始到……终止。

10.5 写作范例(Samples)

- **合同 (Contracts)**

Sample 1

Employment Contract

Wuhan Institute of Shipbuilding Technology (hereinafter called "Party A") wishes to engage the service of Henry Black (hereinafter called "Party B") as a foreign teacher. On the basis of friendly negotiation, both parties agree to sign this contract and pledge to fulfill conscientiously all the obligations stipulated in it.

1. Party B's after-tax salary will be RMB 3,500 per month. The period of service will be from September 1st, 2020 to August 31st, 2021.

2. Party A's Obligations

2.1 Party A shall provide Party B with necessary working and living conditions.

2.2 Party A shall conduct direction, supervision and evaluation of Party B's work.

...

3. Party B's Obligations

3.1 Party B shall observe the Chinese law, decrees and relevant regulations.

3.2 Party B shall observe Party A's regulations concerning administration of foreign teachers and shall accept Party A's arrangement, direction, supervision and evaluation with regard to his work.

3.3 Party B shall complete the teaching tasks as scheduled and guarantee the quality of work.

...

4. Neither party shall revise, cancel, or terminate the contract without mutual consent.

5. One month's notice to the other party is required in case of earlier termination of the contract.

6. This contract takes effect on the date signed by both parties and will automatically expire when the contract ends.

  This Contract is signed at Foreign Affairs Office, Wuhan Institute of Shipbuilding Technology, in duplicate, this 21st day of August, 2020, in Chinese and English, both texts being equally authentic.

Party A: <u>Wuhan Institute of</u>   Party B: <u>Henry Black</u>
    <u>Shipbuilding Technology</u>
(Signature): _____ (Signature): _____

译文
例1

聘任合同

武汉船舶职业技术学院(以下简称"甲方")愿意聘请亨利·布莱克(以下简称"乙方")作为外籍教师。双方经过友好协商,决定签署此合同,并保证严格履行合同上所规定的条款。

1. 乙方的税后工资为3500元/月。聘期从2020年9月1日至2021年8月31日。
2. 甲方的义务
2.1 甲方为乙方提供必要的工作设施和居住条件。
2.2 甲方将指导、监督和评估乙方的工作。
……
3. 乙方的义务
3.1 乙方应遵守中国法律、规定和制度。
3.2 乙方应遵守甲方的外教管理规定,并接受甲方对乙方工作的指导、安排、监督和评估。
3.3 乙方将按约定的进度完成教学任务,并保证教学质量。
……
4. 未经双方许可,任何一方不得擅自修改、取消和终止合同。
5. 若一方提前终止合同,须提前一个月通知另一方。
6. 此合同自签署之日起生效,并且于终止之日自动解除。

此份合同于2020年8月21日签于武汉船舶职业技术学院外事办公室,英文与中文各一式两份,具有同等效力。

甲方:<u>武汉船舶职业技术学院</u>　　　乙方:<u>亨利·布莱克</u>
(签名):_____　　　　　(签名):_____

Sample 2

Sales Contract

No: CH2001
Date: May 3, 2021
Signed at: Beijing, China

The Seller: China Pearls Import & Export Corp.
The Buyer: ABC Co., Ltd.

This Contract is made by and between the Seller and the Buyer, whereby the Seller agrees to sell and the Buyer agrees to buy the under-mentioned commodity according to the terms and conditions stipulated below.

1. Commodity:

Commodity & Specification	Quantity	Unit Price	Total Value
Fresh Water Cultured Pearls	150KG (net)	USD50.00	USD7,500.00

With 0.01% more or less in quantity allowed at the Seller's option.

2. Packing: The packing of the goods shall be preventive from dampness, rust, moisture, erosion and shock, and shall be suitable for ocean transportation.

3. Time of Shipment: Within 50 days upon receipt of the L/C which accords with relevant clauses of this Contract.

4. Port of Loading: Beijing, China.

5. Port of Destination: New York City, U.S.A.

6. Insurance: To be effected by the Buyer.

7. Terms of Payment: By Confirmed, Irrevocable, Transferable and Divisible Letter of Credit to be available by sight draft and to remain valid for negotiation in China until the 15th day after the Time of Shipment.

...

11. Force Majeure: The Seller shall not be responsible for the delay of shipment or non-delivery of the goods due to Force Majeure, which might occur during the process of manufacturing or in the course of loading or transit.

12. Arbitration: Any dispute arising from or in connection with this contract shall be submitted to China Arbitration Commission for arbitration in accordance with its existing rules of arbitration. The arbitral award is final and binding upon both parties.

13. This Contract is executed in two counterparts each in Chinese and English, each of which shall be deemed equally authentic. This Contract is in four copies, effective since being signed/sealed by both parties.

The Seller: The Buyer:

译文
例 2

销售合同

编号:CH2001
日期:2021年5月3日
签约地点:中国北京

卖方:中国珍珠进出口公司
买方:ABC有限公司

本合同由买卖双方订立,根据本合同规定的条款,卖方同意出售,买方同意购买下述商品。

1. 货物:

品名及规格	数量	单价	总值
淡水养殖珍珠	150KG(net)	USD50.00	USD7500.00

数量允许有0.01%的增减,由卖方决定。

2. 包装:货物应具有防潮、防锈蚀、防震并适合于远洋运输的包装。
3. 装运期限:收到符合本合同有关条款的信用证后50天内装船。
4. 装运口岸:中国北京。
5. 目的口岸:美国纽约。
6. 保险:由买方自行办理保险。
7. 付款条件:开给卖方不可撤销即期付款及可转让可分割之信用证,并须注明可在装运日期后15天内在中国议付有效。

……

11. 不可抗力:凡在制造或装船运输过程中,因不可抗力致使卖方不能或推迟交货时,卖方不负责任。
12. 仲裁:凡因本合同引起的或与本合同有关的任何争议,均应提交中国仲裁委员会按照该会的现行仲裁规则进行仲裁。仲裁裁决是终局的,对双方均有约束力。
13. 本合同用中英文两种文字写成,两种文字具有同等效力。本合同共4份,自双方代表签字(盖章)之日起生效。

卖方: 买方:

- **协议（Agreements）**

Sample 1

Agreement of Consignment

This Agreement is entered into between Hengtong Co. (hereinafter referred to as the Consignor) and Columbia Co. (hereinafter referred to as the Consignee), on the following terms and conditions:

1. The Consignor shall from time to time ship air conditioners to the consignee on Consignment basis at the prevailing international market prices on CIF terms. The interval between each shipment shall be approximately sixty days.

2. The Consignee must try to sell the consignments at the best possible prices after obtaining the approval of the Consignor as to prices, terms, etc.

3. The Consignor shall at no time be responsible for any bad debts arising out of credit sales to any buyers. Making payments to the Consignor shall at all times be the sole responsibility of the Consignee.

...

7. The Consignor shall absorb insurance premium and warehousing charges up to the date of delivery to customers.

8. This Agreement is written in English, in two originals; each party retains one copy.

As a token of acceptance, both parties have set their respective hands on this 1st day of May, 2021 with understanding and knowledge of the contents stated hereinabove.

Hengtong Co.: _____   Columbia Co.: _____
(signature)   (signature)

译文
例1

商品寄售协议

恒通公司(以下称寄售人)与哥伦比亚公司(以下称代售人)按下列条款签订本协议:

1. 寄售人将不断地把空调器运交给代售人代售。货物价格为市场CIF市价,约隔60天运交一次。

2. 代售人在征得寄售人对价格、条款等的同意之后,必须尽力以最好价格出售寄售商品。

3. 寄售人对赊销造成的坏账不负任何责任,代售人在任何时候均负有支付寄售人货款的义务。

……

7. 寄售人负担货物售出之前的保险费和仓储费。

8. 本协议英文正本两份,双方各持一份。

双方确认上述内容,并于2021年5月1日签字立约,以资证明。

恒通公司:_____   哥伦比亚公司:_____
(签字)   (签字)

Sample 2

LEASE AGREEMENT

NO: CA9872

Date: June 1, 2021

This Agreement is entered into on June 1, 2021, in Wuhan, China, between ABC Co. (hereinafter called the Lessee) and XYZ Co. (hereinafter called the Lessor). Hereby, the Lessor leases to the Lessee and the Lessee hires from the Lessor the commodity described hereunder in accordance with the terms and conditions set forth below.

1. Commodity and Descriptions:

2. Quantity:

3. Rent: On firm bases.

　　Rent per set:

　　Total rent:

4. Shipment:

5. Place Where the Aforesaid Commodity Is to Be Used:

6. Payment:

The total rent shall be paid in two installments, of which one shall be paid by the Lessee to the Lessor after six months from the date of the commodity's arrival at the port of destination, and the other shall be paid by the Lessee to the Lessor after twelve months from the date of the commodity's arrival at the port of destination.

7. Ownership:

The ownership of the commodity belongs to the Lessor, before he transfers it to the Lessee.

...

15. Right of Using the Commodity:

Nobody except the Lessee may use the commodity, but the Lessee shall not allow any other person to use the commodity without the Lessor's prior written consent.

16. Maintenance:

The Lessee shall keep the commodity in good condition at his expense, but the Lessor shall be responsible for the breakdown of the commodity and the Lessee may lodge claims against the Lessor for any losses occurred therein.

17. Duration:

The duration of this agreement is one year commencing from the date of the commodity's arrival at the port of destination.

In WITNESS whereof the parties hereto have executed this agreement in English, in duplicate the day and year first above written, each party retaining one copy thereof.

ABC Co.: _____　　　XYZ Co.: _____
(signature)　　　　　　　　　　　(signature)

译文
例 2

租赁协议

编号:CA9872

日期:2021年6月1日

本协议于2021年6月1日在中国武汉签订。签约一方:ABC公司(以下称承租人);签约另一方:XYZ公司(以下称出租人)。根据本协议,按下列条件,出租人租赁给承租人,承租人从出租人处租赁下述商品。

1. 商品与规格：
2. 数量：
3. 租金：固定价
   每台租金：
   租金总额：
4. 装运：
5. 上述商品的使用地：
6. 付款：
   承租人付给出租人的全部租金分两次支付,每一次于货到目的港日算起6个月后支付；第二次于货到目的港日算起12个月后支付。
7. 所有权：
   在出租人把合同商品转让给承租人以前,其所有权属于出租人。
   ……
15. 使用商品权：
    除了承租人以外,任何人不经出租人书面同意,不得使用该商品。
16. 维修：
    承租人必须自付费用维持商品的良好状况；但是出租人必须对商品的故障负责,并且承租人可就因此而遭受的损失向出租人索赔。
17. 有效期限：
    本协议有效期为一年,自商品抵达目的港日计算。

    兹证明,双方在以上开首语中书明的日期签署盖章。本协议以英文书写,一式两份,每方各执一份。

ABC公司：_____   XYZ公司：_____
（签字）   （签字）

10.6 练习（Exercises）

I. Directions: The following is an agreement. After reading it, you should give brief answers (in no more than 3 words) to the 5 questions that follow.

（Website）Visitor Agreement

Statesman.com is provided to you by Cox Texas Newspapers. This visitor agreement is legally binding（有约束力的）between you and us. Please read this visitor agreement; by using this service, you accept its terms. The Internet is a fast growing medium; we may change the terms of this agreement from time to time. By continuing to use the service after we post any such changes, you accept this agreement as modified.

We reserve the right to deny access to this website, or any service provided via this website, to anyone who violates(违反) this visitor agreement or who, in our judgment, interferes with the ability of others to enjoy this website, or infringes(侵犯)the right of others.

We invite you to send in your questions or comments about this website, or to bring to our attention any material you believe to be inaccurate. Please send such comments, including a copy of any material you wish to discuss to:

Jim Smith

General Manager

Statesman.com

305 South Congress Avenue

Austin, Texas 78704

Phone: (512) 912-2510

Fax: (512) 912-2926   Or e-mail us

1) Who are the two parties to the agreement?

   The provider of the website and its _____.

2) What is meant if you go on suing the service after changes in the agreement are posted?

   It means you have _____ the modification.

3) What will happen if a visitor breaks this agreement?

   The visitor will be denied access to this _____.

4) What are visitors invited to do about this website?

   Send in their _____ about the website.

5) What can visitors do when they find materials on the website inaccurate?

   They can send their comments to _____.

II. Directions: Complete the following contract according to the Chinese given.

Douglass Company (_____)（以下称买方）as one party and Anhui Import and Export Corporation (_____) （以下称卖方）as the other party agree to sign by their authorized representatives, _____ （经过友好协商）, the present Contract under the following terms and conditions:

1) The Seller will arrange and sell 260 sets of drilling machines in the following two fiscal years.

2) The Seller should take care of the _____ (质量、数量、包装和装运).

3) The Buyer should pay the Seller by _____ (不可撤销信用证) and take care of the insurance.

4) Claim shall be made _____ (在货物抵达后10日之内).

5) _____ (任何一方不得违反合同) without mutual agreement.

6) The present contract is written in English, _____ (有效期两年), after which it may be extended, amended or discontinued.

7) The contract was signed on April 14, 2021 in Hefei _____ (由双方的代表).

_____ (Signature) for the Anhui Mechanic Import and Export Co. of the People's Republic of China.

_____ (Signature) for the Douglass Company of New York, N.Y, U.S.A.

练习答案

第1章

1.1.6

I.

October 12, 2021

Dear Mr. White,

  I would like to thank you for interviewing me yesterday for an associate engineer position in your company. I enjoyed meeting you and learning more about your research and design work. The interview strengthened my interest in working for Shell. I believe my education and experience in team work fit in nicely with the job requirements, and I'm certain I could make a significant contribution to the firm over time.

  Again, thank you for the interview and for your time and consideration.

Yours sincerely,
Barbara

II.

March 24, 2021

Dear Prof. Zhang,

  <u>Thank you very much for the kind hospitality you and your wife showed us</u> during our visit to your country. We appreciate being introduced to so many of your friends and the delicious Chinese meals we had together. <u>Indeed we enjoyed our stay in China tremendously.</u> We arrived in New York safe and sound yesterday morning.

  My wife and I are looking forward to the pleasure of playing host to you and your wife in the U.S.A. <u>We would like to get a chance to return your kindness.</u>

  Please do not hesitate to write to me if you want me to do something for you in the U.S.A. <u>With best wishes.</u>

Yours sincerely,
Mike

III.

April 22, 2021

Dear Hu Wen,

On behalf of my whole family, I wish to express our heartfelt thanks for the New Year's present that you give us. We appreciate very much not only the gift itself but the friendly feelings.

May we, in return, express to you our very best wishes for your health and happiness in the coming year, and also for further success in the project you are conducting?

Thanks to good friends like you and again for the lovely gift.

Yours truly,
Li Ming

1.2.6

I.

November 23, 2021

Dear John,

It was a delightful surprise to hear the news of your upcoming marriage to Miss Alice Black. Congratulations! She is such a clever and beautiful girl and you two are a perfect match. We beg your acceptance of the enclosed gift as a token of our best wishes.

Our best regards to you and your bride once again.

Yours sincerely,
Lily

II.

June 28, 2021

Dear Ellen,

<u>How delighted I am when I hear that you are going to graduate from Fudan University</u> and get a Master's Degree! Though I cannot go to Shanghai to join in the celebration of your graduation owing to the long distance between the two cities, yet <u>I wish to express my most earnest and ardent congratulations through this letter.</u>

For years you have made unremitting efforts in your specialized field and your diligence and intelligence at last win your honor. I am not only happy for but also proud of you from the bottom of my heart.

I believe as an up and coming person, you will use your head and hands to develop your career to a higher level after the graduation.

May you achieve greater success in the future!

Yours sincerely,
Li Ming

III.

Dear Zhang Dong,

It was with great pleasure that I read of your promotion to the position of sales manager of Huawei Company. Congratulations!

I am sure your company has made a very wise decision and that you will excel in your new role.

Please accept my congratulations on your promotion again and my very best wishes for your continuing success.

Sincerely yours,
Wang Fang

1.3.6

I.

June 23, 2021

Dear Mr. Barker,

Mrs. Phyllis Nash, your Personnel Officer has told me that you have a vacancy for a Marketing Assistant. I would like to be considered for this post.

As you will see from my enclosed résumé, I have been a shorthand typist in the Marketing Department of Enterprise Cables Ltd. for two years. I have been very happy there and have gained a lot of valuable experience. However, the office is quite small and I now wish to broaden my experience and hopefully improve my prospects. My present employer has written the enclosed reference and has kindly agreed to give further details if you are interested in my application.

I am able to attend and interview at any time and hope to hear from you soon.

Yours sincerely,
Jean Carson

II.

June 22, 2021

Dear Sir,

<u>I was interested by your advertisement for</u> a Sales Manager in yesterday's *China Daily* and <u>should like to be considered for this post.</u>

<u>My full particulars are shown in my enclosed résumé</u>, from which you will see that I <u>have had 12 years' experience</u> in the sales department of two well-known companies. I thoroughly enjoy my work and am very happy in Phoenix Plastic Ltd., but feel that the time has come when my experience in marketing has prepared me for the responsibility of full sales management.

<u>I shall be pleased to provide my further information you may need</u> and I look forward to hearing from you.

Yours faithfully,
Li Ming

III.

July 24, 2021

Dear Sir,

Having just completed a course in Business Management in America, I write to enquire if you could offer me an appointment with the administrative staff of your renowned establishment.

From my attached résumé, you will see I have worked with some American business firms in various capacities and have acquired considerable knowledge of business affairs and office management. I am eager to practice my newly acquired skills.

I hope you will consider my application and I look forward to meeting you.

Yours faithfully,
Li Qiang

1.4.6

I.

July 4, 2021

Dear Sir,

I really hate to complain, but one thing is really disturbing me.

You might remember that on April 20 we placed an order with you for 50 pairs of sports shoes, emphasizing at the time that the ordered shoes should be delivered before May 20. Unfortunately, the shoes just arrived today about 16 days late. This delay has put us in a very difficult position.

We trust that there will be no repetition of this problem.

Yours truly,

Wang Fan

II.

December 23, 2021

Dear Sir or Madam,

I am writing the letter to complain the camera I bought from your store last month when I was on business trip in Guangzhou. There I took some pictures, yet, when I had it developed after I got home, I found no pictures printed at all. I feel very frustrated about it.

I have posted the camera back to you and strongly insist you refund me as soon as possible.

Yours sincerely,

Wang Lan

III.

Oct. 12, 2021

Dear Mr. President,

My name is Li Ming, a freshman of the Shipbuilding Engineering Department. I venture to write a letter to you about the canteen service on campus which has given rise to a lot of complaints among students.

The focus of the complaint is the poor quality of the food. The vegetables are so overcooked as to lose their nutrients. The price of the food is surprisingly high. Besides, the attitude of the service staff to the students is not hospitable at all.

All in all, there is still much room for improvement as far as the canteen service is concerned. I do hope you could look into the matter as soon as possible.

Thank you for your consideration.

Sincerely yours,
Li Ming

1.5.6

I.

Dear Jasmine,

I am very sorry that I was out when you came to see me yesterday morning.

I had told you that I would be available that morning. However, my father suddenly had a heart attack, and I had to take him to the hospital in a hurry. Had that not happened, naturally I would have been with you. I hope you will not leave the city this week, and I will call on you this Friday afternoon at three o'clock. Please wait for me in your hotel at the appointed time.

Once again, I sincerely hope you could understand me and accept my apology.

Yours,
Chris

II.

February 17, 2021

Dear Mr. Winston,

<u>I would like to apologize</u> for the mix-up on your last order. We recently <u>hired a new sales person</u> who was not familiar with your systems. We have <u>corrected your order and shipped it out</u> this morning. We have applied a 10% discount on your order, and again <u>apologize for any inconvenience this may have caused you</u>.

Yours sincerely,
Paul Cordero
Customer Service Manager

III.

>   July 4, 2021
> Dear Tom,
>   I would like to express my apology that I can't meet you at the airport.
>   Yesterday I was informed that I must attend an important business meeting on the day when you arrive. I will give a speech at the meeting and it is supposed to be over at 11:00 a.m., which will be two hours later than your arrival time.
>   I will meet you at your hotel as quickly as possible after the meeting. I'm sorry again for the inconvenience.
>
>   Yours truly,
>   Li Ming

1.6.6

I.

> Dear Professor Scott,
>   On behalf of the CHI Computer Society, I would be very pleased to invite you to attend and chair a session of the forthcoming conference on Information Technology. The conference is to be held in Shanghai, China, from August 10 to August 13, 2021.
>   We sincerely hope you could accept our invitation. Since you are an internationally acclaimed scholar in this field, your participation will be among the highlights of the conference.
>   You will receive further details later, but we would appreciate having your acceptance soon so we may complete our agenda.
>
>   Sincerely yours,
>   Zhang Hua

II.

>   March 17, 2021
> Dear Mr. and Mrs. Taylor,
>   As the parents of the bride, I would like to <u>take this opportunity to invite you to the wedding of our daughter</u>, Sandra Green to her fiancé Adam Locke. On this joyous occasion,

we wish to share the day with our closest friends and family members.

The formal event will be located at the Fire Lake Country Club on the fifteenth of August at three o'lock, two thousand and nine.

Please RSVP by the fifteenth of June to ensure attendance. We hope to see you there, to enjoy this special day with friends and family.

Sincerely Yours,
Margaret Green

III.

Apr. 2, 2021

Dear Mr. Anderson,

I am writing on behalf of the English Department to invite you to give a lecture on English Literature in our college on Saturday, April 11.

We know that you are a famous scholar in this field. As English majors, our students would like to know something about English literature. We would be very grateful if you could give us a lecture.

If you can come, please let us know as soon as possible. We look forward to the opportunity to benefit from your experience and wisdom.

Yours truly,
Wang Hai
Assistant of the English Dept.

1.7.6

I.

Dear Sales Manager,

We have seen your advertisement online which aroused our great interest in your sportswear.

Please send us a catalog and price list of your products. It would also be appreciated if you could include your terms of payment and inform us how soon you can arrange for shipment upon receipt of our order.

We used to purchase these products from other sources. We may now prefer to buy from your company because we understand that you are able to supply larger quantities at more attractive prices.

Thank you for your assistance and we are looking forward to your early reply.

Yours sincerely,
Michael Smith
Purchasing Manager

II.

Dear Sir,

<u>We received your promotional letter and brochure today.</u> We believe that you would do well here in the U.S.A. Kindly send us <u>further details of your prices and terms of sale</u>. We ask you to <u>make every effort to quote at competitive prices</u> in order to secure our business. <u>We look forward to hearing from you soon.</u>

Yours sincerely,
Alex Grey

III.

Sep. 19, 2021

Dear Sir,

We have seen you advertisement in the magazine, and we are interested in your silk garments. Would you please send us details of your various ranges, including sizes, colors, prices, and some samples?

When quoting, please state your terms of payment and discount you allow on purchases of large quantities. If your quality is good and the price is reasonable, we will place a large order with you. Looking forward to your prompt reply.

Yours sincerely,
Robert Miller
Purchasing Manager

1.8.6

I.

Dear Sir,

Thank you for your inquiry of Dec. 15 concerning our company's laptop computers (Model AS100). It gives us great pleasure to send along the technical information on the model together with the catalogue and price list.

There is a heavy demand for our products which we are finding it difficult to meet. But if you place your order within the next ten days, we make you a firm offer of delivery by the end of December.

We look forward to the opportunity of cooperating with you.

Sincerely yours,
William Roberts
Manager

II.

November 24, 2020

Dear Sir,

Thank you for your inquiry of Nov. 22. In compliance with your request, we included in this letter our quotation sheet for velvet curtains No.21 and 22. As to the relative samples, we have dispatched them to you by separate airmail.

Our velvet curtains are of good quality and moderately priced. As our stocks are low and the demand is heavy, it's hoped that you'll send us your orders as early as possible.

Awaiting your esteemed favors and orders.

Yours faithfully,
Han Hui
Sales Manager

III.

Sep. 21, 2021

Gentlemen,

Many thanks for your letter of September 19. We appreciate your interest in the silk garments produced by our company.

  We are enclosing a copy of our terms of business, where you will find details of our quantity discounts and price list for the products. Also by separate post, we are sending you some samples.

  We hope our products will meet your requirements, and look forward to the opportunity of performing our reliable services.

Yours truly,
Li Qiang
Sales manager

1.9.6

I.

June 22, 2021

Dear Mr. John Smith,

  We thank you for your letter of June 17 and are pleased to place an order with you as per our Order Sheet No. 1324. Provided that the price will remain unchanged.

  Enclosed please find Our Order Sheet No.1324.

Yours faithfully,
(Signature)
Ding Zhiwen
Purchasing Manager
Cindy Garment Co.

II.

Dear Mr Li,

  <u>We thank you for your quotation of your July 13 letter about the laser printers</u>. We are so interested in your products. <u>We decided to place an order with you for 15 printers (Model MP983)</u>, provided that <u>you will offer after-sale service</u>. Enclosed please find <u>a check for $22,500</u>. Please give us reply as soon as you receive our letter.

Yours Sincerely,
John Smith.

III.

Zhongshan Middle School
143 Zhongshan Road
Haidian, Beijing, 400060

Feb. 20, 2021

Dear Mr Li,

    Thank you for your letter of Feb. 16. We are interested in your new type of recorder, AW-501. We are pleased to order 10 sets of this type provided that you could cut down the price to ￥530 for each. If so, we would go and visit you on Feb. 26. Is the date suitable for you? Your immediate reply will be appreciated.

Yours truly,
Li Ming

1.10.6

I.

Dear Sir or Madam,

    I am writing to recommend one of my best friends, Zhou Botong, for this post. With his outstanding leadership and cheerful personality, he was elected chairperson of the Student Union of Tsinghua University several times.

    Busy as he was, he completed his major, teenage psychology, with an outstanding school record. Upon graduation he was assigned to be a teacher in Tsinghua Middle School. What is more, he loves his job and enjoys working with children. This won him great popularity among his students.

    Therefore, I do not hesitate to recommend him as an ideal candidate for the post you advertised. I am sure you will make a wise decision in hiring him.

Yours sincerely,
Li Ming

II.

> July 21, 2021
>
> Dear Sir,
>
> <u>I am very pleased to recommend Miss Li Dan for acceptance to your company</u>.
>
> <u>I have known Miss Li for three years</u>. Throughout that time, she has shown herself to be a <u>hard-working and talented</u> staff member of our company. Miss Li has received professional training in Australia and the U.S.A., and her expertise in her own field is unquestionable. She is an imaginative and at the same time very practical person. <u>Miss Li is kind and popular among her colleagues</u>. She is a well-liked and valuable staff member of our company, and my colleagues all speak highly of her dedication to her work. We are in fact very sorry to lose her.
>
> <u>I strongly recommend her to you without any reservation</u>.
>
> Yours sincerely,
> Li Ming

III.

> Dear Sir or Madame,
>
> It is with great pleasure that I write to recommend Li Ming to you. I have known him for the past two years and have had the pleasure of having him in our History Department. Frankly speaking, he was one of the most outstanding students. And I found him to be a bright, diligent, friendly young man. Besides, Li Ming is not afraid of hard work. And he has a strong ability to negotiate and organize. I believe he is qualified for the job and will do it better.
>
> I strongly recommend him and appreciate your favorable consideration of his application.
>
> Sincerely Yours,
> Professor Leah Kim
> Oxford University

第 2 章

2.4

I.

Announcement

Dear students,

  Please be quiet and I have an announcement to make. We will hold an English lecture from 3:00 p.m. to 5:00 p.m., Wednesday, September 25. The speaker is Dr. Jacob. He is an American teacher. The main content is about classic roles in Western movies. After the lecture, Dr. Jacob will answer relevant questions on-site and he is willing to answer questions about oral English learning. On the occasion, please ask questions and express your ideas without hesitation.

II.

A.

NOTICE

  In order to improve our oral English, we are going to have an English speech contest. It is to be held at 2:30 p.m. May 5. The place for the contest is the activity center for college students. The topic of the contest has no limits. Those who would like to join in the contest are required to register for it before April 15. All students are welcome to attend.

Student Union
April 4

B.

THE PUBLIC COURSES OFFICE NOTICE

July 4, 2021

  All staff from the Department of Public Courses are requested to meet in the department's conference room at 2:30 p.m. on Wednesday, July 15 to discuss next term's teaching competition.

C.

NOTICE

Dear Guests,

 Due to the renovation of the hotel swimming pool, swimming services cannot be provided tomorrow. Other entertainment items can be used as usual. For more information, please call 1866. We apologize for the inconvenience.

Wuhan Hotel
Aug. 7, 2020

D.

Notice

 At the request of the university students, the student union invited Mr. John Wilson, human resources manager of ABC Company, a famous multinational company, to give a lecture to all students.

 Content: How to stand out in the interview

 Time: 7:00-8:30 P.M., June 10

 Location: Library Activity Center

 Participants: All students, especially fresh graduates

E.

Ladies and gentlemen,

 May I have your attention, please? Tomorrow there will be a visit to different places, which are the East Lake, the Yellow Crane Tower and Wuhan University. Those who are willing to go please register at the Service Desk before 10:00 p.m. today.

 We will set out after breakfast at 8:00 in the morning and come back at 5:00 in the afternoon. We will have lunch at the place we visit.

 That's all. Thank you.

F.

a. written permission

b. submit

c. the Personnel Office

d. the following Monday

e. department manager

G.

Announcement

About 35 American students will visit our school from 9:00 a.m. to 13:00 on June 22nd. In order to welcome them, we are going to gather at the gate of our school at 8:40 a.m.

From 9:00 to 10:00 we will hold a welcome party at the reception room. In this party we can give gifts to each other.

In the next hour we will show them around the campus, the library, the laboratory and the language laboratory.

At around 11:30 we will have lunch in the student canteen, and at 13:00 we will say goodbye to them at the gate.

第 3 章

3.4

I.

A.

Lost

A blue Huawei mobile phone

Last seen in the canteen on the morning of July 20, Friday

If found, please call: 13012345678

B.

Announcement

　　Effective from January 1, 2021, the telephone number of Wuhan Sunshine Co., Ltd. will be changed to 027-87654321.

　　Address: No.1 Xueyuan Road, Hongshan District, Wuhan

　　Postcode: 430070

C.

Announcement

　　In order respond to the municipal plan, on and after October 1, 2022, the address of our company will be changed to No. 801, Yanjiang Avenue, Jiang'an District, Wuhan. Welcome to the new address.

Sunshine Software

D.

> Contributions Wanted
>
> The newspaper for the whole staff of our company issued on 1st of each month is now accepting contributions with the contents required as the following:
>
> a. report in each department;
>
> b. advice and suggestions in the production, distribution and sales promotion of our company;
>
> c. the spare time life of our staff;
>
> d. something else available.
>
> And your contributions are wanted no more than 1,000 words. If we won't adopt your contributions, we'll send them back to you in three months.
>
> If you'd like to share your contributions with your fellow colleagues, please contact Editor Yang in the Public Relations Section.

第 4 章

4.6

I.

① F ② F ③ T ④ T ⑤ F

II.

Part-Time Job Offer

Part-time English home tutor wanted

Requirements: CET-6 passed, patient, good communication skills, teaching experience

Contact: Miss Xiao

Phone: 027-86855432

III.

On Sale—English Course Books

Some English course books are waiting for their new owners!

This is a collection of College English books ranging from book 1 to book 4 with CDs attached behind. Many useful articles, either interesting or thought - provoking, are incorporated in the books, followed by some practical and diversified exercises. Therefore, it is of great use to help you pass CET 4 and can also be a good choice of self-study aside from being textbooks.

Considering being used once, they are not brand new, with some necessary notes on the margins. Therefore, they are not charged high, only 10 yuan for each book. There will be a discount of 15% and a surprise gift offered to you if you buy them altogether.

English plays a critically important role in our college study as well as in society. I hope you won't miss this good chance to buy some useful books at a low price. If you are interested, please call 13345678900.

第 5 章

5.6

I.

To: Margret@sohu.com
From: Jim@sina.com
Subject: Congratulations
Date: March 19, 2019

Dear Margaret,
  I read in the morning paper that after five years work in a Sino-American joint venture, <u>you are going to start a business firm of your own</u>. Most impressive!
  I would like to add my congratulations to the many you must be receiving. <u>I'm sure your business firm will be a great success</u>. I sincerely hope you will find in this new venture the happiness and satisfaction you so richly deserve.
                                Jim

II.

Date: 2021-10-1
From: WangDong@qq.com
To: White@gmail.com
Subject: Welcome to Wuhan

Dear Mr. White,
  I am Wang Dong from Hongxia Trading Company. Welcome to Wuhan! I am very glad to do everything I can to help you enjoy a good stay in Wuhan.
  I have reserved a room for you in Optics Valley Kingdom Plaza. There is about 42 kilometers from the Tianhe International Airport to the hotel, and you may take a taxi or the shuttle bus from the airport.

After arriving at the hotel, you may take a rest first. It is advisable that you come to my office the next day and we will talk about our business.

If you need any help, don't hesitate to call me.

Yours sincerely
Wang Dong
Hongxia Trading Company

III.

Date: Oct. 21st, 2021
From: liming@163.com
To: amanda@hotmail.com
Subject: Thank you for buying the book

Dear Amanda,
  This is Li Ming, book salesperson in the ABC ONLINE BOOKSTORE. Thank you for buying the book *Secret to Success* in our bookstore recently.
  I'm writing to tell you that the book you ordered have already been sent out. You can expect to receive it within a week.
  I wonder whether you would like to evaluate our service on the Internet after you receive the book.
  Moreover, I would like to recommend you another new book in the store called *Twilight* and welcome you to buy books from here again.
 	
<div align="right">Sincerely yours
Li Ming</div>

第 6 章

6.1.7

I.

(1) B (2) C (3) A (4) E (5) D

II.

MEMO
TO: All Department Managers   **DATE:** March 14, 2018   **FROM:** Manager of Human Resources   **SUBJECT:** ANNUAL STAFF RETURNS   All Department Managers are reminded that the Annual Staff Returns are required to be at the Personnel Office by 30 January. If there are any difficulties, please inform me.   <div align="right">Signature</div>

III.

Memo
To: All staff   **From:** Kelly Smith   **Date:** April 28, 2021   **Subject:** Nomination of Sales Manger   I am delighted to announce that Mr. Bill Thomas has been nominated as Sales Manager of the headquarters. He will be on duty next Monday. Since he is a new employee, all the members of the headquarters should get prepared to give him a welcome ceremony.

6.2.6

I.

PHONE MESSAGE	
From: David Wolen	**To:** Karl Thomson
Company: Health and Safety Council	
Message: Has confirmed First Aid course beginning on May 13, but can only take 25 participants not 29.	

II.

From:	Wang Jun
To:	Zhao Gang
Date:	Sep. 9th
Time:	6:00 a.m.
Telephone number:	86×××42
Message:	Tomorrow your class will go to Bayi Farm and help the farmer with the apple-picking. You'd better put on your old clothes. You will meet at the school gate at 6:00 a.m. Don't be late.
Signature:	Zhao Ming

第 7 章

7.6

I.

Hu Bin

86 Heping Road, Dalian

Liaoning Province, China

Tele: 0411-66654320

Job Objective

A position related to the shipbuilding

Education and training

March to July 2009	Professional training on shipbuilding in Harbin Engineering University, with a training certificate
July 2007	Graduated from Wuhan Institute of Shipbuilding Technology, majoring in Shipbuilding and Repairing

Work experience

Sep. 2009 to present	Engineer
	Dalian Shipbuilding Research Institute
July 2007 to Feb. 2009	Assistant engineer
	Dalian Shipbuilding Industry Co. Ltd

Personal Data

Born:	March, 1989, in Dalian, Liaoning Province
Sex:	Male
Health:	Excellent
Marital state:	Single
Interests:	Singing, playing football and traveling

References

References are available upon request.

II.

简 历

李西哲

武汉大学975号信箱

湖北省武汉市(430005)

座机:027-87688789

移动电话:13271269603

电子邮箱:lxz2009@sohu.com

求职目标
大学英语教师
学习经历
2002年至今　　　　　武汉大学外国语学院
　　　　　　　　　　英语语言文学硕士(今年七月可获得学位)
1999年——2002年　　武汉第五中学
社会经历
2008年八月　　　　　北京奥运会志愿者
2003年——2006年　　武汉大学外事办兼职口译
2002年——2004年　　校英语报编辑
证书
2006年　　　　　　　英语专业八级考试证书(TEM 8)
　　　　　　　　　　TEM 4 口语考试证书
2005年　　　　　　　国家计算机等级考试二级证书
获奖情况
2008年　　　　　　　获"三好学生"称号
2007年　　　　　　　获2007年全国大学生英语竞赛一等奖
2005年　　　　　　　政府奖学金一等奖
2004年　　　　　　　英语戏剧比赛二等奖
兴趣爱好
听音乐、旅游、绘画、书法
个人资料
性　　别:男
婚姻状况:未婚
出身日期:1983年12月23日
健康状况:良好

身　　高：178cm
体　　重：65kg
其他资料
备索
III. 略

第 8 章

8.6

I.

Cinnamon Leaf Oil

Ingredients: Cinnamon leaf oil and other inflammation reducers

Functions: For bone & muscular aches, fracture swelling, sprains

Administration: <u>External use only</u>. Apply and rub over affected part frequently

Warnings: <u>Avoid direct contact with eyes</u>

Shelf life: Two years

Storage: Keep tightly sealed in cool place

II.

芬必得胶囊

适应证:缓解多种原因引起的严重疼痛和肿胀

用法与用量:吞服,一次一粒,早晚各一次

注意事项:12岁小孩用药请咨询医生意见。用药过度可致头痛、呕吐

有效期:3年

储存:置于阴凉干燥处

第 9 章

I.

王经理的时间表	
11月2日（星期一）	
上午8:30	约见怀特先生
下午4:30	去机场接布莱尔先生
11月3日（星期二）	
上午9:30	带布莱尔先生参观工厂
下午2:30	和布莱尔先生讨论合同
11月4日（星期三）	
上午9:00	写总结报告
下午4:00	参加公司职员大会
11月5日（星期四）	
上午10:00	去艺术馆看展览
下午2:30	参加商务会议
11月6日（星期五）	
上午9:00	送布莱尔先生去机场

II.

Annual General Meeting of Shareholders of Sino-America LJ Computer To be held on December 10, 2021 at Wuhan Mayflower Hotel, 385 Wuluo Road, Wuhan, China. TEL: 027-68871588	
Time	Agenda

8:30 a.m.-8:45 a.m.	Registration
8:45 a.m.-9:00 a.m.	Opening Ceremony
9:00 a.m.-9:15 a.m.	Welcome & Introduction
9:15 a.m.-10:00 a.m.	Report of the Managing Board on the 2020 financial year
10:00 a.m.-10:45 a.m.	Report of the Supervisory Board on the 2020 financial year
10:45 a.m.-11:00 a.m.	Coffee break
11:00 a.m.-11:30 a.m.	Allocation of profits
11:30 a.m.-12:00 a.m.	Question time
12:00 a.m.	Adjournment

第 10 章

10.6

I.

1) visitor/user
2) accepted
3) website
4) questions or comments
5) General Manager/Jim Smith

II.

  Douglass Company (<u>hereafter referred to as the Buyer</u>) as one party and Anhui Import and Export Corporation (<u>hereafter referred to as the Seller</u>) as the other party agree to sign by their authorized representatives, <u>as a result of friendly negotiation</u>, the present Contract under the following terms and conditions:

1) The Seller will arrange and sell 260 sets of drilling machines in the following two fiscal years.
2) The Seller should take care of the <u>quality, quantity, packing, and shipping</u>.
3) The Buyer should pay the Seller by <u>irrevocable L/C</u> and take care of the insurance.
4) Claim shall be made <u>within 10 days of goods' arrival</u>.
5) <u>Neither party shall break the contract</u> without mutual agreement.
6) The present contract is written in English, <u>valid for two years</u>, after which it may be extended, amended or discontinued.
7) The contract was signed on April 14, 2021 in Hefei <u>by representatives of the two parties</u>.

  _____ (Signature) for the Anhui Mechanic Import and Export Co. of the People's Republic of China.

  _____ (Signature) for the Douglass Company of New York, N.Y, U.S.A.

参考文献

[1] 王达金,余勤.大学英语写作、翻译考试绝招[M].武汉:湖北科学技术出版社,2004.

[2] 晨梅梅.实用写作教程[M].上海:上海外语教育出版社,2008.

[3] 黄爱良,周游,张淑标.高等学校英语应用能力考试(A级)全真试题精解[M].武汉:武汉出版社,2008.

[4] 章振邦.新编英语语法教程[M].上海:上海外语教育出版社,1983.

[5] John Langan.美国大学英语写作[M].北京:外语教学与研究出版社,2001.